To [signature]

Hope this Book meets all of your expectations of who the Boys in the window really are

Good Luck and Good Reading

[signature]

THE BOYS
IN
THE WINDOW

WRITTEN BY

JOHN BOURGEOIS

A Story About The Social Habits Of Elderly Gentlemen.

Copyright 2010

Forward

Walk into any coffee shop, fast food restaurant, or shopping mall food court, usually in the morning and you will see elderly people sitting together socializing, and sharing their family events, their excitements, and their tragedies. Mostly, these are today's baby boomers. Some are retired, some are unemployed, and some are actually still working. These people represent the largest portion of today's population.

They come together with all kinds of histories and experiences. They are representations of today's diverse ethnic backgrounds, education, work environments and social status'. However, in most group situations and settings, those differences are set aside; some are diminished, or even overlooked from one another, as they gracefully age.

Some of these people harbor prejudices that have been deeply rooted within the makeup over their lifetime, and they cannot always be expelled. No matter what their age, these prejudices sometimes come to the surface, as you will read herein, but all of these people share some commonalities they all identify with.

Foremost is that is that they are all getting older. They're aging, and their bodies don't do what they want them to do anymore. They have come to the realization, that death is just a matter of time. They might even tell you, it's not the tragedy one would think, but more like the inevitable. Let's face it we're all going to die sometime, they'll say.

It's just that the elderly have accepted this fact, while the younger folks have not, and some actually think they're going to live on forever, there will be a cure developed for their ills, and it's not going to happen to them.

Introduction

In the town of Dungeon Rock, Massachusetts, every Saturday and Sunday morning a group of elderly gentlemen meet and greet each other while they sit inside the front window of a local coffee shop.

They are a closely knitted group, and they only know each other from this coffee shop, and meeting place. Sometimes they do meet outside this shop with the occasional rendezvous to the local sports bar to watch a game, or to the local golf course here and there. But the majority of the time is right here in this coffee shop window.

They have become members of the world's philosophers, a special group of old folks, who have been everywhere, and seen it all. Each day they attempt to solve all of the world's problems, and sometimes they think they actually do!

Although members of the group come and go over the years, they all give each other support and advice, as they age gracefully together. They share their maladies and celebrations with each other, as well as their successes and failures. And while they all come from varying backgrounds and experiences, they each have their own unique personalities.

They hold high regard, and respect, for the life learned expertise each one of them brings to the morning "roundtable", while they develop a special relationship of respect, and love for one another, although they do talk about each other when one of them is not there. No one is exempt from this chattering of gossip.

This fictional account is an attempt to give respect and insight into the daily activities of what their interaction with one another is. The younger folks might say, "What's up with them? They're always here, every time I come in here." Well this might help answer that question.

When you see these groups you might ask yourself "What is the great attraction?" Hopefully when you read this account, you might get an idea of what brings them together. The bottom line is that we can all look forward to a similar camaraderie of people, and places like this, in our futures. So remember that thought, because you'll be there soon enough!

Chapter 1   *Around the Town...*

A small North Eastern city located just north and adjacent to The North Shore, Dungeon Rock has a population of about thirty-five thousand. It has no real industry, so to speak, and is located in an urban area that used to house large shoe manufacturing plants and large textile mills around the turn of the 20th century. But these industries have all moved overseas, and the area is now largely a seaside resort community.

There are however, plenty of churches, restaurants, and schools in this quaint city. It is an average, or typical, upscale suburban community. The only real claim to fame it has, is that it was the childhood area of Walter Brennan, Tammy Grimes, Harry Agganis, and Tony Conigliaro just to name a few. This is where they studied, played and prayed. Most of the people who live here are professionals, i.e. doctors, lawyers, stockbrokers, teachers, bankers, artists, and others.

There is a downtown area comprised of a historic theatre called the Causeway Emporium. It is located directly across from the quaint public library, which is a colonial styled building with large white columns and a red brick exterior. There are also many banks in this town. It seems there is a bank on just about every block. No one seems to know why this is. It just is.

The local city hall is just to the south of the railroad tracks that drive right through the center of town. It is another red brick building with large white columns, white trimming and ornate windows. It is this style of architecture that makes the town attractive and nostalgic.

Located between the library and City Hall is a small commuter rail stop and train station anxiously waiting for the suburban daily commuters to begin their daily trek into the big city. Commuters have plenty of choices of where to go to get their morning cup of coffee, to take with them on the long train ride down town.

There are at least four coffee shops within walking distance of the train platform with numerous restaurants dotting the main streets that enjoy much patron activity. From the early hours of the morning, until way after the sun goes down, there is plenty of foot traffic to these shops.

The small local police station is located in the basement of the City Hall building, but there isn't much crime here, other than teenage mischief, and the once in a while bicycle theft. A few years back some folks tried to get a new police station built, but the majority of the people just did not want to spend the money on something that they felt wasn't needed. The people here are very conservative, and resistant to change. They like things to stay the way they are.

There are two churches in this central area, and many other shops, from shoe stores, to clothiers, to dress shops. As small as this town is, the downtown area supports many local small businesses, including a bagel shop, a bakery, and at least ten other restaurants and food establishments, all within walking distance from one another. It is what makes this town attractive to tourists and very trendy.

Shoppers have no problems finding a place to eat. It is one of these shops that our story begins on an early Saturday morning. As the sun rises, while the dew evaporates and the town now comes alive to breathe in the influx of the people who will enjoy it.

Our story begins at one of the coffee shops situated along the main street, overlooking the rush hour traffic, in the wee hours of the morning.

Chapter 2 *The day begins...*

Back at home he lay there with his eyes closed, trying to get the energy to get up and begin his day. As he lay quietly he thinks to himself. He's sixty-seven years old, and he is winding down to retirement, but it's just not time yet.

The alarm on the radio has gone off softly, and the morning news is now quietly playing next to him on the nightstand. He has been listening to this news station for most of his life, and it tends to start his day. Beside him lays his wife, fast asleep. He can hear her peaceful breathing, so he knows she is okay. She stirs momentarily as he gets up, and turns over on her side.

The time is five AM and the sun has not risen yet. He struggles to get up into a sitting position on the side of the bed. He then slides his legs over to the side, and while stretching his arms out, and yawns. He whispers quietly "Whoa Boy", but catches himself, and looks over towards his wife to see if she has awakened. She stirs a little but immediately settles down, and he gets up and quietly walks into the bathroom across the hallway.

He thinks to himself how stiff his joints are, from being motionless through the night, and how the pain will subside as the day goes on. His medications will help him ease the pain and he'll shortly be on his way.

As he stands in front of the mirror, he rubs the top of his head with both hands to wake himself further. While running the water in the sink, to splash on his face, he'll wipe away the sleep that he has accumulated through the night. Next he'll get his pills. He keeps them in the linen closet next to the bathroom sink. He's not on any prescribed medicines though, but he does take a vitamin supplement, fifteen hundred milligrams of Glucosomine Chondroitin, and eighty milligrams of aspirin daily. He firmly believes they help avoid health problems, easing his joint pain, and protecting him from a stroke or heart attack. He's not much different that any other elderly person these days, when it comes to self-medicating.

After this brief awakening ritual, he opens the medicine cabinet in front of him. He reaches in and takes out the toothbrush and toothpaste then closes the cabinet door. While pausing to stare at himself, in the mirror, he wonders where all the years have gone. He brushes his teeth, and combs what hair he has left. Next, he shaves the stubble that has grown on his face from the day before, and cleans his razor under the running water.

This is the morning ritual he has done day after day, year after year all of his life. This is his start of the new day, and he does it each morning while giving thanks, that he has good health, that his good wife is OK, and that he is somewhat financially secure and ready for whatever the future is ready to bring.

He'll now get dressed and head out of the house to meet the "Boys" at the local coffee shop. He's come to realize that his wife would be sleeping for at least another two hours. It would then take here additional time to get up, and get ready to do anything with him, or go anywhere. So he ventures out on his own, and he'll meet up with her later. Putting on his overcoat he heads out the door, being careful not to let it slam behind him.

As he leaves he makes sure that the door is locked and secure. He wants to leave his home knowing that his wife of thirty years is safe and secure so he double checks everything whenever he leaves.

The garage door opens slowly as it is cold, as things seem to slow up in the winter, including him. He is also somewhat slow, while he gingerly walks the driveway, as he has done numerous times before. He enters the garage and gets into his late model sedan.

He slips the key into the ignition; it starts up right away. He puts on the radio to finish listening to the news, as he backs out of the driveway for his short ride to the coffee shop. On the way there, he looks up at his mirror and notices the temperature display. It says it is twenty-eight degrees outside, and he can hear a faint beeping noise, indicating an "icy roads" warning.

When he gets to the shop, he cautiously proceeds to the parking lot, securing a spot next to the entrance door. He is the first to arrive as the shop opens and greets him, its first customer of the new day.

It is now 6 AM on Saturday morning. It is a little chilly outside today. The sun is now starting to rise. Inside the shop the front windows are now showing some signs of daylight. There is a slight dusting of snow on the ground outside. The city's snowplows creep slowly by, with their blades raised high in the air, laying a new bed of salt, on the town's paved thoroughfare.

Of the four tables the shop has set up against the front window, the second one is where the hub of activity takes place. The coffee shop is well situated and functional, with full windows running the entire length of the building. Each table can accommodate two people. However, the patrons move and rearrange this seating to their personal preferences all throughout the day. The tables against the windows are square, while the ones slightly away from them are round. They can comfortably seat three or four when it's needed.

Being the first to arrive, Rick carries with him a newspaper, slung under his arm. The paper was in his doorway when he left home that morning. It is his morning copy of Barron's Daily, an investor's newspaper specializing in the stock market and trading areas.

He is a schoolteacher by trade, teaching the eighth graders science and math. But he's also a part time investor. He will show up about this time every Saturday morning, and a little bit later on Sundays. He is a tall thin gentleman in his late sixties with balding hair and glasses. He is usually dressed very neat with slacks and a dress shirt, sometimes a tie. It is evident that he has spent some time primping for his morning venture out into public. He is now ready to greet the world.

Rick is a very sociable gentleman, with an eye for the ladies, who personally greets each and every one of the shops female customers, whether he knows them or not. Whereas he only greets male customers when he actually knows them personally.

Always sitting at the same table, he instinctively occupies the same chair. The other participants, that will join him later, feel funny sitting in that seat when he is not there. It is known as Rick's chair. He's even been referred to as the "Mayor" of this local coffee shop and he fulfills the role very well.

His mannerisms are predictable and always the same. Being a student of finance while in college, Rick has a definite interest in the daily activities of the stock market. So his instruction guide is his latest issue of his Barron's newspaper.

Earlier in another part of town, it's four AM when the alarm goes off. She reaches over to silence it and buries her head back into the pillow and pulls the covers back up. But a few minutes later the alarm sounds again and she realizes it is time to get up and get ready for work.

She jumps into the shower and stands there under the hot steamy water, relishing the warmth and wishing she could get back into bed. But no, she has become resigned to the fact that if she is to succeed in life she must grow up and get off to work to help pay the college tuition her parents could not afford.

The days are long for her. She dries herself off and realizes that her uniform is still downstairs in the drier. She rushes down to retrieve it and put it on. There is no time for make up; she'll have to do that in the car on her way to work. She is running so late now. She'll only have time to dry her hair, put on her clothes and be out the door. It's tough being twenty-two and burning the candle at both ends. But she must have some social life, she thought to herself.

She had to clean off the snow from her windows and warm up the car. "It is so cold in here", she uttered. Putting the car in gear she's on her way to begin her daily routine. "Why did I have to take classes on Friday?" "Because it was the only night they offered it", she thought. Normally, when her Friday class ended at 6:30, she was off to the local eatery, to catch up with her friends.

She should have gone home after dinner, but no her friends insisted they go line dancing, and that is what did her in. She knew she had to start work at five but she went anyway. So now she is not only tired, but is sore from all the dancing activity. She was thankful though that she did not drink. If she did, there was no way she was going to get to work in the morning.

"Oh good, stopped by the morning train." she thought as she reached into her purse for some lipstick and eye shadow. She was right in the middle of applying it, when the gates went back up. She tried to finish up, when someone from behind her blew their horn. She looked up into the rear view mirror and grimaced.

She threw her stuff back down on the seat next to her, and proceeded to go. She angrily stepped on the gas bouncing rapidly over the tracks and leaving the car in back of her way behind. "The nerve of them, it's only four-forty five in the morning. Where the hell are they going this early that they're in such a hurry?" she thought.

She turned into the parking lot and parked way in the back. She grabbed her lipstick and makeup from the seat, and put it into her purse. She'd need it later. She locked the car and ran in through the employee entrance, walking directly behind the counter, while saying hello to the other workers, as she hurriedly walked by. Now all settled she started to prepare her cash register for the day.

Glancing at the clock it was close to five thirty AM. She went and unlocked the front door; retrieved the coffee containers from the dispenser, and brought them over to the coffee station, where the customers would pour their favorite flavors of coffee. She then went back to behind the counter and waited for the first customer to arrive.

When Rick enters the shop, his routine is the same every day. He walks into the shop, and greets the counter clerk. He then sets his paper down on the table, and takes off his coat, while draping it across the back of the chair. He walks over to the counter and orders a small coffee but because the shop wants to increase their sales, they do not keep the small paper coffee cups in view. They instead keep them under the counter, so as to not encourage the sale of small coffees.

The Clerk behind the counter is Nancy and she has been there for a few years. As part of the store's uniform, and for health department regulations, she wears a baseball cap on her head that has the coffee shop logo on it. She also wears an apron. She is always works the weekends while saving up her money to make ends meet.

One thing though, she always has a smile and a good attitude when dealing with the customers and her coworkers. As Rick approaches the counter she greets him. "Good Morning sir, how can I help you?" She looks Rick up and down and notices his paper on the table.

Because he is a regular customer she makes small talk with him and asks him what's the hot stock of the day. He tells her that now is not the time to buy stock. Now is the time to hold any stock that you have. There is too much uncertainty in the market right now. She shakes her head up and down as she listens to him, fully knowing she has no money to buy stock, and is just making small talk with him. "I'll have a small coffee in a paper cup." He states. The clerk displays a face of displeasure, while reaching under the counter for the small cups.

She fishes around for one and places it in front of him. "Here you go sir, that will be a dollar fifty-nine." Rick reaches into his pocket and digs deep. He has some change in each pocket. He pulls out a handful of change, and meticulously counts out the amount, so as not to over pay. "Here you go! You have a nice day now." Rick grabs the cup and proceeds back to his table. "Yes sir, I sure will, you too."

With that, Nancy goes back to her business of readying the counter for the day's customers. She has fresh bagels that just came out of the oven and she has to get them off of the racks and onto the displays. Then there are fresh baked breads she'll do the same with, but before she does that she'll take all of the left over breads and bagels, and put them in a large plastic bag. These will go to the guy from the homeless shelter. He picks these up each morning and distributes them to their overnight guests. There is a lot that goes on around here, she thought.

Chapter 3   *Let the rituals begin...*

Rick takes his cup, walks over to the coffee station, and fills it with the Light Roast blend. He is careful not to fill it too much, so he doesn't spill it on the way back to the table. When he gets there, he puts the cup down next to his newspaper. Predictably his cup is placed in the same spot next to the paper each and every time. He is not obsessive compulsive, but everything has it place for making oneself comfortable. He turns and walks to the back of the shop.

In the back of the shop, and next to the employee entrance door, is a soda machine for the customer's use, but it also dispenses cold water and ice. Rick always gets a plastic cup and fills it with ice water. They'll be a lot of talking today, and he'll need the water to stop the dryness in his throat during these, sometimes, heated and laborious discussions.

After he fills his glass he walks back to the table, being careful not to spill any. Sitting down and squirming in his seat to get comfortable, he picks up the newspaper with both hands and opens it up to read. Then he states, with a bit of frustration and boredom. "Whoa Boy!" which is a habit of his that he's unaware the he has, but it is evident to all others that it's a favorite phrase he uses to start a conversation going. However, this time, there is no one else there so he continues to read his paper.

It is three thirty in the morning when the alarm goes off. Jack does not have to be anywhere in particular, but he does have to take the dogs out. He can hear them calling him from down stairs. They're telling him they need to go out and go out now! Jack jumps up and puts on his pants and shirt and goes down to tend to the dog. When he comes back in prepares himself some cold cereal and listens to the news on the radio as he waits to bring the dog back in.

With the dog back in the house, he jumps in the shower and starts priming himself for the day. It is Saturday and he'll wear nothing special, just jeans and a shirt. It is now about five thirty and he goes down stairs and logs onto his computer to check for any emails.

"Better start a load of laundry before I leave," he thought. So he grabs the laundry, puts it in the washer and starts the machine. He is now ready for the day. "Hmmm, let's see am I forgetting anything, dog, laundry, dishes in the dishwasher, nope nothing else," he thought to himself. He put on his coat and walked out the door and started his truck. He leaves the driveway and proceeds down the street, when he realizes he forgot his laptop.

The coffee shop has a wireless connection that lets him log onto the Internet. He is the information guy in the group. He is their lifeline to the verification of the accuracy of their statements. He's like the unofficial referee. So he turns his truck around, and heads back to the house to retrieve his most precious possession. Shortly, he is back in the truck and on his way to the shop.

Jack enters the shop carrying his case containing the computer. He's much shorter than Rick and is also overweight. He is clean-shaven, and wears his hair slicked back. He's also nearsighted and wears glasses. So he's always putting them on, or taking them off, as he looks at the computer screen or elsewhere.

When he enters the shop, Rick glances up at him and starts to move his things around the table so Jack has room. "Hi Jack, How is it going?" Rick yells from across the room. "Morning Rick! Its going well, hope you had a good week." He continues to walk over to Rick's table and places his case on it. He removes his coat and drapes it on the chair's back, and walks back over to the counter.

All the while, the clerk just watches and smiles. She knows Jack is a regular customer, but gets annoyed at the way he places his order. He has an obsessive, compulsive personality, and things must be done in the same order, each and every time. The Clerk watches as Jack approaches the counter. "Good Morning sir, how can I help you?"

"Yes, I'll have a medium coffee in a paper cup, and give me a sesame seed bagel, and can you slice it on the bread machine, and can I have two butters, and can you put it on a small tray, and can I have a real knife instead of a plastic one?" Jack replies.

Nancy listens attentively and gives an exasperated look, rolling her eyes, as she briefly glances at Rick, while smiling back at Jack. She has heard this order each time he comes in to the shop. It never changes. She wonders if this guy has any variety in his life. She even wonders if he knows the shop sells other things. "Has he ever looked up at the menu board?" She is very patient though and says "Why of course sir. That will be two ninety-eight." With a smile on her face she begins to take his money and prepare his order.

Jack reaches into his pocket and pays the clerk. Grabbing his cup and tray, he walks back to the table sets the tray down, goes back over to the coffee station, and fills his cup with their Dark Roast blend. He always adds half and half cream to lighten it, puts a cover on it, and goes back to the table where Rick is waiting.

Taking his computer out of its case he sets it up and logs onto the Internet. "Did you see what Stepan Chemical stock is selling for?" moans Rick.

"No, I don't follow it anymore, since I'm not with that company anymore." replies Jack.

"It's up to sixty-two dollars a share. What was it when you told me to buy it?"

"Twenty-three." replies Jack. "Whoa Boy! I should've bought it then." Rick states with remorse.

Jack continues to work on setting up his computer. He comes to the shop certainly for the socialization but also for the use of their wireless Internet. Since he has been out of work for so long, he can no longer afford to have it at home, so he uses wireless wherever he can find it.

At this moment there is a silence in the shop. With the exception of the background music, there are no conversations taking place. Rick is busy reading his paper, Nancy is busy cleaning the counters and Jack is engrossed in his computer. He's lost in the Internet world, that so many people are addicted to these days. He'll search job board after job board only to submit application after application.

He understands that the way HR departments scan resumes today, they can easily weed out an individual because of their age, and he firmly believes he's not getting interviews because of this. But he keeps plugging along, hoping there is something out there for him and that he'll get a call soon.

Meanwhile Rick changes the pages on his paper. He holds it up to stretch it out, and smooth the pages so it is easier to read. Jack continues fiddling with the computer and starts typing, when Rick interrupts him. "I can't believe it, twenty-three dollars then; and sixty-two now. That was only a year ago. What was it last month Jack? Go ahead, look it up." Jack looks up from his keyboard and down again. He starts typing to get the answer to the question. "It was fifty-eight dollars" he replies.

As this conversation ensues, a female customer walks into the store, and over to the counter. She stands in front of Nancy who is waiting to serve her. She is an attractive woman in her thirties, tall with blonde hair gently covering her shoulders. She is physically fit and quite attractive. She walks to the counter and glances over at Rick and Jack sitting nearby. She comes into the shop quite frequently and she always sees the two of them sitting in the same place. She doesn't know them personally, or outside of the shop.

Rick nods and acknowledges her presence. "Hi, how are you doing? Good to see you." Rick states as the unofficial coffee shop greeter. She nods in reply with a slight smile. She's placing her order to Nancy when another customer comes in and stands somewhat away from the counter, but behind the first woman waiting her turn to order. She is also a young female in her mid twenties, slightly shorter than the woman in front of her. She's wearing a white ski coat and black slacks and suede boots. The boots have exceptionally high heels on them.

Culturally, there seems to be an invisible line embedded in the floor of the shop about five feet from the counter. You would think so because when ever customers come into the shop they seem to stand behind that invisible line if someone else is already at the counter.

As she is standing there, she notices both Rick and Jack sitting at the table. She glances over at them, while walking to the counter. "Hi, how are you doing, good to see you?" says Rick. Jack does not say anything and goes back to working on his computer. She smiles and retorts back. "Good morning, sir." Rick smiles because he has just received verbal acknowledgement of his existence from a beautiful young female. He feels good now. It makes his day all worthwhile.

Just then a third customer walks in, a young businessman. He is carrying a briefcase, and wearing a black fedora hat, and a long overcoat. He has a scarf draped around his neck, and expensive winged tipped shoes. As he approaches the counter you can hear the heels of the shoes as they meet the floor. "Click, click, click." He glances over at the table, as he walks to the counter. Rick sees him but doesn't say anything. Jack never takes his eyes from his computer, and is unaware of the man's presence, and continues what he was doing.

Chapter 4   *The controversy...*

The next customer to come in is called Dr. Doom. Not much is known about this person, only that he comes in regularly. He is a tall thin gentleman of about sixty-years old. Most of the time he wears black jeans, a black fitted t-shirt, with a New York Yankees logo on it with a black leather Harley Davison motorcycle jacket complimented by heavy leather gloves. To compliment this he always wears dark wrap around sunglasses. In the winter he drives a small subcompact auto, but he would prefer to be on his motorcycle all the time, and can't wait for warmer weather to arrive.

He's not a doctor at all. He received the nickname of Dr. Doom because he is so mysterious, and seems to come out of the shadows.

No one knows much about him. They don't know where he lives, nor do they know where he goes when he's not there. What they do know is that he worked for years at a chemical company, but the company was sold, he was let go. This more than five years ago, and he's not worked much since. Just lives off of his severance and retirement package.

He's too young to collect social security, so he works part time driving a hotel shuttle bus back and forth from the local airport. His real name is Jim. They only call him Dr. Doom when he is not there, because he's always gloomy. To his face they just call him Jim, when he's gone its Dr. Doom. He's tall and slender, and has a psychological problem concerning the natural aging process, mainly his own, meaning he wishes he were still young and back in his forties or even younger.

In those younger years he must have been quite the ladies man. To compliment his looks he wears a cheap hairpiece. He thinks it makes him look younger. He bought it off of the Internet on E-Bay. He really believes it looks good on him. Unfortunately, it doesn't fit his head right, and he's always adjusting it, when no one is looking.

Everyone is afraid to tell him the truth, so they just deal with it. After all, it's his head.

His normal attire is dark clothing. Today he is dressed in black jeans, dark t-shirt, and a long dark wool trench coat. In his hand he carries a large cup of coffee that he bought from another coffee shop, across the street. He doesn't like the coffee at this shop, but we think he does like the company because he's always here. Or could it be that the women who come into this shop are more attractive than the ones who go across the street. No one really knows for sure.

As he walks into the shop he doesn't say a word, and walks directly past Rick and Jack. He heads to an adjacent table and sits down. Peering out of the store's window from behind the sunglasses, he blankly gazes across the street. He is never been seen without his dark sunglasses. The glasses just add to his mysteriousness. His stare is calculating. What could he be thinking, one asks? He doesn't say anything, just sits with legs stretched outward, cup in both hands, and gazes out through the glass.

Rick nudges Jack and says, "What's with him?" Jack just shrugs his shoulders in a gesture of not knowing. "Did we do something?" Jack doesn't reply and goes back to his computer. "Morning Jim?" states Rick, as Jack looks up from his computer screen looking towards Dr. Doom. "Hey Jim, how is it going?" adds Jack.

Dr. Doom sits up, and slowly takes a sip from his coffee, puts the cup down, while still holding it between his hands. He always has both hands wrapped around the cup, as if he was praying, but the cup was in the way to divert what his actual activity is. In a deep, but very soft voice, almost inaudible, and as if he didn't notice their presence, he turns his head towards them. Seemingly disinterested he acknowledges their presence with "Oh, hi", then goes back to staring out the window, at the shop across the street.

Throughout the morning, customers come and go. If it is a female customer the men notice her presence. If it is a male customer they continue amongst themselves unnoticing. Just then another male customer walks into the shop. None of them say a word. The customer walks over to the counter, and is cheerfully greeted by Nancy, who takes his order. When done ordering, the man grabs his tray, and proceeds to the back of the shop.

The next to arrive is a shapely young female customer. She is in her early forties, and has on a tight fitted red sweater, with gray dress slacks. Over that she has a dress coat with the front opened and allowing one to see her tight fitting sweater beneath it. She is carrying a Kate Spade purse and is wearing high heel shoes that click on the marble floor as she walks across to the counter.

Because of the noise on the floor as she walks, all of the old gentlemen listen closely. They certainly can hear her strut. They look at her as she approaches the counter. Rick and Dr. Doom scan her up and down, and then glance at each other. They give her a second look, but this time more carefully. She looks towards the two men while Dr. Doom suggestively removes his sunglasses, giving her a nod of his head. She knows she is being looked at, and struts towards the counter with more exaggeration in her hips, as she looks at the group. "Hi how ya doing, good to see you!" says Rick.

The woman nods and smiles briefly, acknowledging their presence. Jack never looks up still staring at his computer, while Dr. Doom turns towards Rick, holding his sunglasses in his hand. Dr. Doom looks away at her, and then at Rick. He is dying to enter into conversation with the group, but does not know how to engage them so he utters. "You know, those Yankees may just do it this year!" speaking to no one directly, while placing his sunglasses back on the top of his head.

He continues, all the while inspecting the woman out of the corner of his eye. "Are you kidding? They don't stand a chance." States Rick. He continues. "They did it one time, a few years ago, and you Yankees fans think it'll happen year after year. Well it isn't going happen again! The Red Sox have a much better team. Better hitting, better pitching, and better fielding! Overall their record is much better, and they have a better chance than anyone in the league."

"You're crazy! The Yankees have better records in all areas!" Dr. Doom states, so everyone in the place can hear his commanding voice. Rick looks over to Jack, who is busy on his computer.

Jack is not much of a sports follower, and could care less about the Red Sox or the Yankees.

All he knows is that he lives in a town that has strong opinions of these two teams. If you live on the North side of town you're a Red Sox fan and if you live on the South side of town you're a Yankees fan. The only team he is interested in is the Cubs because that's where he grew up, but even so, he'll only follow them if they make it to the playoffs, which has not happened in many years. Rick utters a command to Jack. "Jack, Look it up!"

Jack is in the middle of typing something. He glances up at Rick and gives him an annoyed look. Jack continues typing something, and then hands the computer over to Rick. "See, it says right here, their batting averages were higher; they're pitching ERA's are lower, and their fielding percentage is much better. They are a much better team." Rick boasts.

"Oh ya? Well, who won more games last season, huh! Who got into the playoffs huh! Not your famous Red Sox?" Dr. Doom angrily replies.

There is a silence from the men, as if the argument is over, but it isn't, and will continue at a later time. Right now Rick will let the heat of the moment cool off, as he can see Dr. Doom is getting very irritated. Dr. Doom and only a handful of patrons in the shop are Yankee fans. It's always a hot topic, as to which is the better team. It is one of the subjects that these old men wrestle with time and time again, and it will continue later. But right now it's time to change the subject, thought Rick.

Chapter 5   *Romantic interludes...*

After practicing law for many years Louie has semi retired. He is twice divorced, and lives in a two-bedroom condominium in a high-rise downtown building located in an adjacent town. Each morning it's the start of a new day for him. He has had two heart attacks, a pacemaker installed, three major surgeries, an artificial knee, and hip, and testicular cancer, not counting his broken heart from the lack of romance.

He is seventy-six years old and still yearns for the companionship of a woman. He's not picky though with his criteria for his ideal mate. They must be smart, and they must be thin, he always says. He has signed up to numerous dating services, and overall has not had much success. But he does have his prospects though.

It is early Saturday morning at the Colonial hotel in Danvers, MA. Louie has just stepped out of the shower and reaches for a towel to dry himself off. He checks himself out in the mirror and begins his grooming ritual. When this is done, he dresses in slacks and a dress shirt. He reaches over for the phone next to the bed and makes a call. Sitting on the bed, he cradles the phone to his ear and begins to put on his socks and shoes.

His overnight bag is all packed and he's ready to checkout "OK, then I'll meet you in the lobby in a few minutes, after I check out, then we'll get some breakfast, if it is OK with you." He smiles after hanging up the phone, and scans the room so he didn't forget anything. He closes the door behind him and walks to the elevator, suitcase in hand. Upon reaching the lobby he sees his companion. He greets her, and together they walk to the hotel counter to check out.

As they sit in the hotel restaurant, Louie orders bacon and eggs, over easy, with whole-wheat toast, coffee and juice. "You know that's not good for you" she says, "You should have fruit and cereal instead." "I know, but I'm so hungry after dancing all night. I wasn't sure I'd get up this morning. I was so tired."

"Alright, this time, but next time it's the fruit and cereal, OK?"

Louie looks at her and has a big grin on his face. "You mean there is going to be a next time?"

"We'll see" she retorts.

After breakfast they each get into their separate cars, and head out for the long ride back to their respective homes. She is heading home, but Louie's got other plans. He's heading for the coffee shop. That's the place where the boys will be, because, after all, it is Saturday.

Louie is known as the Liberal Lawyer because of his political posturing. Hell, he doesn't posture at all. He is very opinionated about his views, while most of those in the group are staunch conservative republicans, and Louie is the only strong liberal democrat. He's always ready to forcefully put forth his liberal ideas, consistently trying to get the group to change their views to his way of thinking.

In the early sixties while attending law school, Louie was an active member of the Students for a Democratic Society. Also known as the SDS. He was your typical hippie type, with very curly long hair. While in the SDS he participated in many demonstrations against the Vietnam War. He was also there at Kent State in Ohio during the National Guard shootings. Through his involvement and activism activities, he knew Abbie Hoffman, Jerry Ruben and the others of the infamous Chicago Seven.

He was one of the principal organizers for the camping that took place in Chicago's Grant park, and was there when the riots happened at the Democratic National Convention, and helped the acquaintances of the Black Panthers in the Fred Hampton defense case. He grew his political opinions on the Liberal side of the house. He's sorry he missed Woodstock. These activities helped formulate is present political view on how things should be done in our society today. He's very proud of his activist activities.

Louie pulls his black BMW 565, into the parking lot of the coffee shop, parks it carefully, and gets out, walking into the back door, or rather the employee entrance to the shop. As he enters, with a big grin on his face, he walks directly to the front of the shop where the group is gathered.

He's wearing his black Greek Fisherman's cap, and a Navy style pea coat, he bought from where else, but the local Old Navy store. He is very proud of these clothes, although no one knows why. They think he thinks it makes him look dashing!

While he walks over to where the group is sitting, the big grin he wears never leaves his face. It is an exaggerated grin. Sometimes it looks as if he is in pain. Rick looks at him, as do the others. "Hey Louie, what are you smiling about?"

"He must have gotten something else for free! You know those Liberals, always wanting something for nothing." Dr. Doom injects.

"He looks like the guy with the big grin on his face in the TV commercial for the male enhancing drugs." Says Jack with a laugh in his voice." The rest of the group also laughs with Jack.

Louie doesn't say anything and continues to grin. He quickly raises and lowers his eyebrows a few times in succession, as if he knew something they didn't. Louie walks over to an adjacent table and pulls from his pocket a paper coffee cup, and sets it down. The group, of old men look at him. "Did you see what I just did?" states Dr. Doom. Rick and Jack together, affirm by nodding their heads. Louie does not acknowledge their remarks and continues with what he was doing.

He removes his jacket and cap and places them on an adjacent chair, grabs the cup and walks over to the coffee station. He begins to pour his cup of coffee. All the while Nancy, the clerk behind the counter, is keeping a watchful eye. She looks at the group and raises both hands into the air and shrugs her shoulders. She again looks towards Louie, and then at the group. Her body language is saying "What the heck?" but she says nothing.

After pouring his coffee, Louie walks back to the table and sits down.

"WELL?" says Rick.

"I got Lucky last night?"

"You got lucky? I don't believe it. You've had two heart attacks, an Angiogram in your artery, a stent put in, your supposed to have a pacemaker installed, and you got lucky? If that ever happened you wouldn't be able to tell us. We'd know, because we would've read about it in the newspaper. That is, in the obituary column." States Rick.

Dr. Doom doesn't like Louie that much, and seizes any chance he can to put him down. "Ya, he got lucky all right, he woke up this morning and he was still here. That's lucky, for him," snidely retorted Dr. Doom, while the entire group of old men roar with laughter.

"Hey Louie, Rick told me you had a hundred dollar bill pinned to the bottom of your bedspread with a safety pin. What's that all about? When he told me I didn't believe it, so I wanted to hear it right from the horse's mouth!" said Jack.

"Look, I live alone, and I come here every day. The money pinned to my bedspread is a reward. It's so if you guys don't hear from me, one of you can come over to my condo, and see if I'm all right. If I'm dead in the bed, then the one, who finds me, gets to keep the hundred bucks." The group, of old men are roaring with laughter now.

"OK, enough of that. Let's get back to you getting lucky!" asks Rick.

"Well, truth be told, I went out of town with my new girl friend, and we went to the Colonial hotel in Danvers, and we stayed the night." said Louie.

Just then, a female customer walks into the shop and approaches the counter; she glances over at the group of old men. "You mean to say you were both..." Rick interrupts his conversation and looks at the woman at the counter, as do all of the others in the group. She turns and looks at her audience. "Hi! How are you doing, good to see you?" Rick states. Rick continues with his comments to Louie. "In the same room?"

"Well not exactly. She was up there for a workshop, so she already had her room booked. Her room was included in the price of the conference. I was just lucky that the hotel had a vacancy so I could get my own room. We did have dinner together though," stated Louie.

"See, I told ya so. But he sounds more like a stalker! Wherever she goes, he's sure to follow. Wait a minute! Isn't that Mary Had A Little Lamb?" said Dr. Doom. The old men roar with laughter again, but they are even louder now.

"Well at least I'm making progress!"

"Yes, you're making progress all right. From no dates, to some dates. Pretty soon it'll be DO dates. Like, Louie DO this, and Louie DO that, and Louie drive me here, and Louie drive me there. You might as well be married again." States Dr. Doom.

"Hey it works for me! Did you guys see the movie, AVATAR?"

"No, not yet, but I'm not sure if I want to." Said Dr. Doom.

"It made more money than Titanic," replies Louie.

With a quick and authoritarian reply Dr. Doom states. "No it didn't!"

Just a soon as the words leave Dr. Dooms lips Louie replies. "Yes it did!"

Dr. Doom gets more agitated. You can see the veins in his neck popping as he speaks. "I'm telling you, it didn't. You snuck in and saw it for nothing, didn't you? So how can it make money if all the liberals around the country like you, do the same thing?"

Rick is getting uncomfortable at the two men arguing and steps into the middle of the conversation. "Jack, look it up, so we can stop this bickering."

Jack looks up at Rick and then begins typing on the keyboard. He pauses for a moment to view the screen and then hands the computer over to Rick.

"Well technically you might both be right. Because as of last weekend, it didn't, but it should by this weekend because it is only shy by 7 million dollars of surpassing Titanic. So let's call it a draw". Rick hands the computer back to Jack, who puts it down and goes back to typing.

Jack looks up from the keyboard and says to Louie. "So you saw AVATAR did you? What else did you see? Because I know how you go to the movies! You buy one drink, free refills; one popcorn, free refills; and you bring the newspaper column with the show times, so that once you pay and get in; you can go from movie to movie without paying again, and you spend the whole day there. That's why you always see every movie out there way before the rest of us even get a chance."

"See, I told you so. Those liberals want everything for nothing. Free housing, free health care, free food stamps, and they want all us taxpayers to pay for it," said Dr. Doom.

Louie brags "What's wrong with that? Why, I even have my own set of glasses for the 3D Imax, besides, why do you want to deny everyone free healthcare? Everyone in the group looks puzzled at each other, with their hands raised, as if to ask, "what's this have to do with the subject at hand?"

Dr. Doom is getting very angry now. His face is turning red. He removes his sunglasses, and puts them down on the table and says. "There you go again, bringing up your agenda, which has nothing to do with what we were talking about."

Rick tries to control the conversation and bring it back to decent level, so he tries to change the subject. "How is the market doing? Jack, look it up!" Jack looks back down at this computer keyboard and begins typing. He pauses for a moment, and looks back at Rick. "Up by 20 points."

"Great, I bought some shares of Microsoft the other day and I wonder how they're doing? Jack, look it up!" Jack looks back down at his keyboard and begins to type.

"Crap" he says. "Dam internet knocked me off again, now I have to freaking reboot the thing, and start all over. Boy that pisses me off when this happens. Hang on this is going to take me a minute." They all wait in anticipation of Jack coming up with the answer.

It is nine-twenty in the morning and he has just returned from his walk around the condo complex where he lives. He is a short man of about five foot five, with gray hair, now turning white. He still has some original color visible by the dark streaks running through it. His eyes are recessed and dark and his skin is tanned. It does not matter what time of the year it is, his skin always has an olive tone to it. As he enters his condo he can hear the TV in the background, he yells from the back door. "Turn on twenty-six, I want to get the market report."

From another room his wife loudly replies. "Stock Market, Schmock Market, all you do is go out for your walks, then sit in front of the TV, and all day long you stare at that ticker thing running across the bottom. You'd think it was the tape of your EKG, and you're wondering if you're still alive. Why can't we be like normal people and go somewhere on Saturday mornings?"

"Well get your coat on and we'll go to the coffee shop" he states.

"Sure we'll go to the coffee shop, where I get to sit alone and you get to sit with all of the old farts, and talk about the stock market, no thanks! I'll stay right here, thank you. You can go by yourself, I'm going to go to the market, not sit around and talk about it!"

When she finishes talking she turns up the TV even louder so she doesn't have to hear him again. He abruptly turns around, and walks out the door.

As he enters his car, he ponders for a moment, before leaving the driveway. He starts the car, and slowly backs out and speeds away.

Before he retired, he was the lead man of a crew on a city garbage truck. He was away from home for long periods of time, spending after work time in the bars, but he was always watching his money. He had a weird fascination of the financial sector, constantly keeping an eye on the markets. His market dabbling was always in small investments, but did provide direction to his pension and 401K plans. He grew these funds into a substantial amount over the years.

Now that he's retired he watches his money even more carefully. He's afraid his additional supplement to his city pension, his investments, will somehow run out of capital, and he'll have to live solely on the pension alone. Sometimes he ponders "why he couldn't have made it in the fight game?" He was after all a golden gloves champion.

When he was younger he fought in the bantamweight class at the park district, but he always wished he were a bigger and stronger man so he could fight in the higher weight classes. He also wondered why his mother named him Nicholas? It was a stigma that haunted him as a child. After all he was Italian, and the name Nicholas was a Greek name. His grandfather, on his mother's side, was Greek and because of that his mother decided to name him after him, Grandpa Nick.

As a kid growing up in the neighborhood the older kids would always pick on him. They would tell him he was not Italian, but was Greek. It bothered him all the time. He grew up on the south side of Boston on Summer Street in a neighborhood that had a mix of Italian and Irish immigrants. There he lived on the third floor of a frame three flat, and developed his wind stamina from running up and down all those flights of stairs each day.

Summer Street was mostly an immigrant Italian neighborhood back in the 1940s. Nicky was always getting into fistfights defending his Italian heritage, especially with the Irish kids. Gangs were not prevalent as they are today. Back then it were more ethnic cultures that stuck together, and if you were not of the same ethnicity, then you were considered an outsider.

No matter what his full name was, he made sure each and every one of those kids called him Nicky. If they didn't, then they'd have to answer to him. This childhood toughened him up. It helped develop the way he sees the world today. It allows him to cope with his never-ending internal struggle.

He goal was to succeed in life, and leave that neighborhood and never look back.

Today has had some financial successes. He drives a large Cadillac Coupe Deville. He believes it to be a success status symbol, and he proudly displays it, wherever he goes. When he comes to the shop he always made sure he parks it across the street from in plain view of the windows. However, you could only park over there after nine, because of the city's parking restrictions. It was always entertaining to the folks inside the shop as he drove up, partly because he was so small; and the car was so big, it was hard to see him behind the wheel. But no one had better say a word about it.

Upon entering the coffee shop, and being a short elderly gentleman of slight stature, Nicky talks with a typical Southy Italian toughness in his voice. When he walks in, he is always the center of attention, but as quickly as he enters the shop, he just as quickly turns around and exits, running across the street as if he forgot something.

While walking across the street, he reaches into his pants pocket for some change. He walks over to a pay phone in the lobby of the pancake house nearby. A short time later he returns and walks back into the shop. You see Nicky does not have a cell phone. Does not believe in them, and thinks that if he had one, someone could tap into the phone, and hear all his conversations. Besides that, technology scares the hell out of him.

Nicky follows the stock market obsessively, investing here and there, but he's not good at it, that's why he relies heavily on his broker. Oh, he sometimes wins, but lately he's been loosing often, but so hasn't everyone else who's in the market.

He walks in and sits down in an empty chair within the group. He doesn't buy anything, nor does he take off his coat, he just sits there looking at Rick.

"Did I overhear you say you bought Microsoft?"

Rick looks back at him. "Yup!"

Nicky pauses and thinks for a moment. "How many shares you buy? My broker says they're supposed to pop pretty soon you know. I'm just waiting for the earnings announcement to come out before I make a move and tell him what to do."

Rick looks around, and leans over towards Nicky. In a soft voice he says. "I know, but I got in on the ground floor and bought." Rick holds up his hand and raises four fingers. Nicky looks at him and states "Four thousand shares?

"No."

Again Nicky asks. "Four hundred shares?"

" NO!"

To which Nicky exclaims! "Are you telling me you bought four shares? Boy you're going to make a killing all right. The broker's fees alone will eat up any profits you might get." The entire group is laughing again, when one of them spills his coffee all over the floor. As usual it was Louie. He quickly gets up grabbing napkins from the table, and starts to wipe it up.

"Why bother Louie, you didn't pay for it anyway!" Dr Doom says with a sarcastic tone, but no one laughs. They just look at Louie, as he wipes up the spillage from the floor. Louie rises up to his feet and walks over to the garbage can to throw away his napkins and paper cup.

"Hey you threw your cup away! You know what that means, you'll have to buy another one next time you come in" said Dr. Doom. Louie does not reply but walks back to the table. He starts to put on his hat and coat, getting ready to leave when Rick says "Leaving Louie?"

"Yep, got places to go, things to do, and movies to see. See ya all next time. We'll have to do this again tomorrow. I can't wait, really looking forward to it. You know, being single, I can't leave here and get this abuse at home, like you guys! I have to come here for it!" Louie says while laughing. More laughter ensues from the group.

Louie leaves the shop, and then Dr. Doom gets up, and with his cup in his hand, and proceeds to walk out of the shop. When Rick see this he states "Hey you all leaving us too?"

"No, you're not that lucky, I'll be right back; I'm going across the street to get a refill on my coffee, since the coffee here really sucks!"

Chapter 7 *Prejudice let Yee rise to the surface!*

After dropping his son off at the train station to go back to college in Indiana, Stu sits for a moment in the parking lot as the train pulls away while listening to the car radio. The traffic report states that there was an accident on Interstate 80, and all of the lanes are blocked. It's the worst traffic jam in quite a while the newsman states. Stu thinks to himself about how he might have been on that road, if it weren't for the fact that he had to be in a meeting at work in the afternoon.

Normally he would have driven his son back to school on Saturday. But Stu, being a construction engineer, was heavily involved with the O'Hare runway expansion project, and there was an important meeting to go to. He just had to be there, and couldn't miss it.

Stu studied architecture and engineering at Peking University in Mainland China before coming to the US after college. He was working at the Chinese Embassy Washington DC on a new construction project and at the direction of the Chinese government. During that time there was a lot of political unrest back home.

His family urged him to stay in the US, and not to return and get caught up in the anti government movement. The communist's were rounding up all present and former students. Stu didn't know what to do. After much thought and viewing all of the news reports on TV, he decided to defect to the US. But if he did this, he would never be able to return to his homeland again. As he was already in Washington, he made a secret visit to the US State Department. After some paper work and interviews the US allowed him to stay, but he had to leave the Washington area.

They relocated him to Wisconsin, where he attended Marquette University, and got his Master's degree in Engineering. He attended a job fair after graduation, and was offered a position in a large architectural firm in Chicago. This was just the beginning of a long and successful career.

Stu worked long hours. His parents had contacts in the Chicago area, and working with their relatives, they arranged a marriage for him. Today he has a wife and two sons, one in high school, and one in a Wisconsin college, his US alma mater.

Stu believes in the educational process, so he encourages his two boys to do the best they can in school. Now with one of them in college, Stu struggles to make ends meet. With tuition costs, and dorm fees, his disposable income has shrunk considerably.

He is a tall thin man, with short black hair, that is thinning now because of the stress and his age. He always dressed in slacks and a dress shirt, and enjoys watching basketball games of any level. As stereotypical as it might sound, he was a former ping-pong champion in China, but he gave that up years ago. He doesn't play anymore, but does like to watch it when he can.

Stu is relieved he isn't driving on the highway today, and decides to go to the coffee shop. It is still early, and his meeting is not until the afternoon.

Stu walks into the shop and looks around. Being the youngest of this group, he's not even close to thinking of retiring. "No gray hair here," he thinks of himself as he looks around at who's there. After entering he immediately scans the interior of the shop. He is looking for a newspaper that someone has left. Stu never buys one if he doesn't have to. It's another expense he doesn't need and at a dollar a copy, it'll help pay for his coffee, by not buying a newspaper. However, there are no papers around today.

He walks over to the newspaper stand, in the back of the shop, near the counter. He takes a paper from the rack and doesn't pay for it. In his mind, he's just using it. He'll put it back later when he's done.

Nicky leans over towards Rick and utters in a soft voice (as he keeps a constant eye on Stu) "Great! Here comes the Jap!" Rick leans back towards Nicky and replies in a soft voice so Stu doesn't hear.

"I told you he's not Japanese, he's Chinese."

Nicky, in a loud voice so all in the group can hear, except Stu. "Ya right. Japanese, Chinese, Cantonese, Burmese, they're all the same to me, he ain't Italian."

Stu proceeds to a table, somewhat away from the group, and sits by himself. He puts the paper down and walks back to the counter to buy a cup of coffee. He then goes to the coffee station and fills it up. Walking back to his chosen seat, he sits down and starts to read the paper. Rick upon seeing where he is going to sit says, "Hi Stu, how's it going?" Nicky just glares, and says nothing, while Jack is busy typing on his computer.

One of the things that really bugged Nicky about Stu is the fact that he never lost his Chinese accent. Sometimes when he speaks fast, you have to listen carefully to understand what he is saying. Most of the time it sound like someone mumbling, and Nicky has no tolerance for that, where the rest of the group just nods in agreement, no matter what Stu is saying. Which causes Stu to exhibit some pretty puzzling looks at times.

"OK Rick, How you doing?"

Rick continues. "Did you watch the game last night?"

Stu responds but because no one has a clue as to what he is saying, they just nod when he speaks. "Yes, I watched it and fell asleep in the second quarter, so I'll have to read about it today. Who won? Oh, here it is." Stu glances down at his paper. Rick doesn't know the answer so he turns towards Jack "Hey Jack, look it up will you!"

Jack types on the keyboard and hands the computer over to Rick who glances at it and hands it back. He can't be bothered to get into this conversation about sports, as he has no interest. As Rick glances at the screen he states. "Looks like Marquette won, good they were due to win"

Stu agrees, as he reads from the paper. "Yeah that's what it says here, had trouble finding it." As the men are engrossed in their activities, which to outsiders might look like they are totally impervious as to what else is going on in the shop, another woman comes in followed by a man. The woman is dressed in a business pantsuit with pinstripes. She is shapely and in her thirties. Most of those in the group recognize her because she has been there many times before. The man behind her is dressed in a jacket and jeans. He appears to be a contractor, with a baseball hat and a pencil behind his ear. They are obviously not together.

Rick acknowledges the woman, but ignores the man. Dr. Doom has returned from across the street for his refill, and walks in behind the two of them. He checks out the woman as he returns to his seat. Carefully sipping from his cup, he trains an eye on the activity at the counter. Constantly watching her every movement. "Hi! How ya doing? Good to see ya" says Rick. He turns his head back, and buries his face in his paper, uttering. "Oh Boy!"

Everyone checks their watches, Jack packs up his computer, and Nicky gets up and walks away. Stu is buried deep in his paper, while Dr. Doom leans back in his chair, stretches out his legs, and gazes out the window at the shop across the street.

"See you guys!" states Rick.

"Ya, see ya tomorrow!" Jack says as he leaves.

Rick is left at his table alone and quiet. Everyone has left, except Dr. Doom. Rick picks up his paper and continues to read while Dr. Doom blankly stares out the front window, not saying a word. Nancy is busy at the coffee station wiping the counter top and checking to see if the creamers and coffee containers need refilling.

Dr. Doom looks over at Rick and states "Well, no use hanging around here. I guess I'll go home and fight with the old lady. I just hope she went out, but I'm usually not that lucky. What time you got?"

Rick listens to Dr. Doom, while looking down at his watch. In his mind he's thinking what kind of life is that? He seems so miserable all of the time. He's probably depressed, but he won't go get any help. Coming here is no therapy. In fact, it more than likely causes you to loose your sanity, with all of the different characters that come in here.

"Eleven forty-five." States Rick

"Well I'm out of here."

"Alright. I'll see you tomorrow." Said Rick.

"I'm not sure if I'll be here, she has to go over to her sisters and I'll probably be going with her. So, we'll see."

"OK we'll see." Replies Rick.

Rick is now the only one left in the shop. He picks up his paper and continues to read. He glances out the window and sees Dr. Doom walk across the street and open his trunk lid.

Dr. Doom takes out two large dumb bells and closes the trunk. He starts to go for a walk, all the while pumping those dumb bells up and down. He walks down the street until he is out of sight.

At first Rick thought this behavior was odd. But then he started putting two and two together. It all started making some sense. Dr. Doom dyes his hair and he wears a cheap hairpiece. He wears the sunglasses to hide the crow's feet around his eyes, and he always wears his motorcycle shirt or jacket. He didn't get his motorcycle until late in life, and he always rides alone.

Rick's analogy was this. Dr. Doom is having a crisis with the fact he is getting old. He's doing everything he can to make himself younger. Which, in his case, is extreme.

It's OK to exercise, but taking two dumbbells with you when you walk? Riding alone, because most of the riders are much younger, and you don't fit in? "Oh well, to each his own," he thought.

Rick folded up his paper and neatly laid it on the table as he got up and put on his coat. He picked up the paper and tucked it under his arm, and started to walk out the door when he heard.

"Good Bye! See you tomorrow." A cheerful voice spewed from behind the counter. It was Nancy waving to him as she watched him leave.

Chapter 8   *Church services...*

It is Sunday morning, and the tables are empty as Jack walks into the shop. He takes the usual table in the window and puts down his computer case, while removing his coat placing it on the back of the chair, then walks back to the counter, and approaches the clerk. It's Nancy working the counter again this morning. She is anxiously waiting for him to approach. "Good Morning Sir, how can I help you?

"Hi. I'll have coffee in a medium paper cup, and can I have a sesame bagel, and can I have it sliced and toasted on the bread slicer, and can I have two butters, and can you put it on a tray, and can I have a real knife instead of a plastic one?"

"Why certainly sir, that will be two ninety-eight." Nancy replies

Jack reaches into his pocket and takes out the money to pay the clerk. In the mean time, the clerk gives him a paper cup and his bagel. She cheerfully tells Jack, "Thanks, and have a nice day!"

He walks back over to the coffee station and fills his cup up and then back to the table, balancing his tray and cup. He places them down, and starts to setting up the computer and logs onto the local WIFI system. He types on his keyboard immersing himself into the screen.

Earlier that morning, Smitty gets up and out of bed. His wife has already left for work a long time ago. She works weekends and he is retired from the Chicago police department. After getting dressed Smitty trots downstairs to his basement. He has a safe sitting in the corner of a spare room there.

Removing a key from his pocket he walks over to the safe, and opens it. There inside is his vast collection of guns and rifles. He removes his

9mm semi-automatic. He checks the breech and magazine, and puts it into the side of his pants under his shirt.

Normally this gun would have been in the nightstand next to the bed, but his grand daughter was visiting last night, and he locked it in the safe for her safety. He just forgot to take it out, and put it back after she left. Now he's fully loaded and ready to go. He grabs his briefcase containing his laptop, and removes his wireless mobile card from the charger on the kitchen counter, and puts it into his pocket.

Then, after setting the house alarm, he locks the door behind him, and walks outside to get into his car, a black 2007 Hummer. It's seven AM and he's on his way to the coffee shop. He sings to himself in the car as he drives down the street. He hates to listen to the news in the morning. The crime just pisses him off and ruins his day. He'd rather hear about it when he gets home at night. So he just hums to himself. After all, he'll be at the shop in a minute.

Smitty doesn't park his car in the coffee shop lot, but instead parks in the public city lot across the street. This way he can keep an eye on it, while sitting in the front window with the boys.

He only wears two things to the shop, either sweatpants and sweatshirt, or Army fatigues, and a fatigue jacket. No matter what the temperature, that's what he wears. When he enters the shop it is an impressive sight. As much as he tries to stand up straight, it is difficult.

Over the last few years he has had some problems with his legs, and his knees are giving out. This causes him to hobble when he walks. You can tell he is in some pain as he sometimes winces when he puts weight on the bad leg.

He should have surgery, but he is waiting for his Medicare to kick in, he's only 64 now. He'll wait another year or so. But he never complains. His pain is visible by the wincing on his face as he walks.

Smitty is a large and tall man, with slicked back gray hair. He has a moustache, and today he's wearing the sweatshirt and sweatpants. Visible and under the shirt is a large bulge on his side. It's the gun he is carrying underneath.

As he enters Jack is busy working on his computer and does not notice his presence. Smitty is greeted by Nancy as she does everyone when they enter. "Good morning sir! How can I help you?"

"Just coffee and a Danish please."

"That'll be two ninety-eight please." She replies.

Smitty reaches into his pocket and pulls out his wallet, and pays with a credit card. The clerk processes the card and hands him a receipt. She gives him the Danish on a tray, and also a paper cup. He walks to one of the tables near where Jack is sitting and places the tray down, and begins to setup his computer. He plugs in his mobile wireless card.

Smitty does not trust the local free WIFI or public airwaves, even though the coffee shop has a free wireless connection available, he'd rather use his own. He says it's more secure and he has a lot of information on his laptop that he can't jeopardize.

"Hey Jack, watch my stuff while I get my coffee, will you?

"Who do you think is going to take it, the Ham-burgler? He works in a different shop, and you're the only retired cop in here, and those aren't donuts on your plate. So I think your safe." Jack says jokingly.

"You never know now, do you? You can't be too careful. Trust me, cause I know!"

Smitty grabs his cup from the table and walks over to the coffee station. With his back to the windows, and where Jack is sitting, he begins to prepare his coffee. Nancy is standing behind the counter watching him, while waiting for the next customer to arrive. Jack goes back to working on his computer.

Outside of the shop, and wheeling his shopping cart by the front window, is a homeless man. He has a lot of over stuffed brown garbage bags draped all over the cart. He is wearing a ragged overcoat and has knitted gloves on that have no fingertips on them. His shoes are worn and they are tied together and hanging off of the cart, while he wears black boots with buckles on them. The buckles are not fastened and they flap as he walks. He stops and peers in through the glass. He has all of his personal belongings, and garbage bags filled with his entire life in them.

As he peers into the window he scans the area to see who is inside. He spies the Danish on the table, and sees that no one is sitting there. He is unnoticed as he walks into the shop over to the table. Jack is busy on his computer and doesn't notice him, while Smitty is busy filling his coffee cup, and doesn't notice him either. But Nancy is just standing there watching him.

All of a sudden, the homeless man takes the Danish off of the tray, and just as casually walks out of the store. He quickly wheeled his cart away, while biting on the Danish, with his boot buckles flapping rapidly as he walked away. Meanwhile, Smitty goes back to his table, coffee in hand, and notices his Danish is missing. He looks around at the other tables and does not see it.

"Ok Jack, very funny, but what did you do with my Danish?"

Jack glances up from his computer and looks puzzled. He hasn't a clue as to what Smitty is talking about and shrugs his shoulders.

"What?"

"You know what I'm talking about. I left my Danish here while I filled my cup. I asked you to watch it. Now I come back, and it's gone. Did you eat it? Because I know you are quite capable of eating it in such a short period of time?"

"Smitty, honestly, I don't know what your talking about. I don't know what happened to it. I'm just as puzzled as you are."

The Clerk just watches the exchange between the two men, and smiles. She is enjoying the small heated discussion between the two old men. She finds it quite amusing. "Excuse me? Excuse me gentlemen!" They are not paying attention to her.

She keeps calling to them when they finally reply in unison.

"WHAT!"

"Well while the two of you were engrossed in your activities, you getting your coffee" pointing to Smitty, "and YOU working on your computer," pointing to Jack. "Some homeless guy, wheeling a shopping cart, came by, stopped right there." pointing to a spot out front, "Then he looked in the window. He walks right in here and over to your table, took the Danish, and quickly left." She exclaimed!

"You're kidding, right?" Smitty asks.

"No sir, I'm not."

Smitty gets up from his chair and looks towards Jack. "Watch my stuff again. I'll be right back. And this time, really watch it will you?"

He tries to run out of the shop, but stumbles because of the pain in his leg. His mind tells him what he should do, but his body doesn't cooperate. He regains his balance and continues out the door. The homeless man is out of sight and nowhere to be found, which is a good thing for him. Had Smitty got a hold of him, there's no telling what might have happened. In any case though there probably wouldn't be any evidence left, based on the way the homeless guy was quickly eating it. Smitty returns back into the shop.

"He got away!"

"Well, it is just as well, because as soon as Louie gets here, and hears about this, he's going to give us a lecture on how if we would have voted for the Liberals, they would have put programs into place providing food for the homeless, and this guy would not have to be stealing Smitty's food." States Jack.

"Ya, and if Louie had his way, I'd put a sign on the front of my house that says FREE BREAKFAST, and I'd feed them all and let this guy have the spare bedroom! That's NOT going to happen!" Replies Smitty.

"Yes, but if the conservatives were elected, they would have lowered the tax rate to businesses, which would then expand their business, therefore allowing them to hire more people, and this homeless guy would have a job, and an income." States Jack.

"Yeah right. Unfortunately, this guy is a crook, and if you followed the Liberal point of view, LIKE LOUIE THE LAWYER, he'd enter my home and rob me blind, and on the Conservative side, he would NOT be working, because, no one would hire a crook. Now...if he came in here and said he was hungry, or held up a sign in the window, I might have given him the Danish." States Smitty.

Jack listens attentively to what Smitty is saying. But because Smitty is normally very opinionated, he's having trouble believing what Smitty is saying.

"You would?" asks Jack

Smitty looks back at Jack, while raising his head to look up at the ceiling. He ponders for a moment before he replies.   In a sinister and sarcastic tone he states, "Naw!"

Just then, Green Lake Willie enters the shop. Now Green Lake is a frequent attendee to these weekend impromptu meetings. In fact he loves to meet with the guys and socialize. However, it's not just this group that he visits on a regular basis. He has another group at the local McDonald's restaurant he's in, another one at Dot's Diner, and he also has a group over at the local Catholic church, where he meets on Sundays just so he can count the collection plate's revenue.

He likes to stick his nose in everyone's financial business. By counting the revenue at the church, he's able to see just how much the parishioners have donated. He relishes in other peoples financial shortcomings.

When he enters the shop he doesn't go to the counter, but instead goes to one of the tables near Jack and Smitty. He sits himself down, and leans his elbows on the table with his hands folded in a praying gesture. He is a short pudgy man in his sixties; he wears a jacket and old man's cap. He doesn't remove them but just sits there, with his fingers interlaced, and smiles. Jack looks up at him and says.

"What are you doing here so early?

"Got to go over to the church and count the money?

"What money?" Interjects Smitty.

"You know, the collection plates."

"Is that why you have a big smile on your face? What time is the mass over?" asks Jack.

"How the hell am I supposed to know? I don't know. I just go there to count the money? It makes me feel good. I like to stack it, hold it, fold it, mold it, and count it. Like the saying goes, "Give me buckets of it. Buckets full of Duckets. Treasure loads full of it. Let me walk around in it. From Missoula, to Eldemeero, I wanna be a millioneerro, give me the money, money, money, money, money, ...Even if it isn't mine."

"Kind of sounds like you got a plan, a scheme, something up your sleeve? Are we going to read about you in the papers?" Asks Jack.

"No, not really, but there are about three or four of us that do it every week. It's kind of like a social occasion. Call it our therapy session. Or better yet, call it our destiny!"

"Ya, like kids on a treasure hunt. Opening the envelopes, seeing what's inside, pulling out the booty. When in reality you guys just want to see how much money each member gave to the church. You're like a bunch of old ladies who gossip. And I supposed any money that falls on the floor is left for the "Sweeper"? Asks Smitty.

Willie quietly sits there, his hands folded, twitting his thumbs, rubbing his hands together, and just quietly smiles back at the two men.

"Hey where's Rick, shouldn't he be here by now? I have to ask him about some investments" States Willie.

"You know what really gets me? You come here all the time, and each Sunday you ask the same question. The same question each and every Sunday. Over and over for years! You come in and you ask, where is Rick, and we give you the same answer each time. "Jack is getting excited as he speaks.

"So?" Willie says with a smile because he knows he is now annoying Jack, and he enjoys the conflict he has planted in the group.

"OK for the umpteenth time. On Sundays Rick has husbandly duties he has to do at home, if you know what I mean. You go to church, loosely speaking, call it his Missionary duties. After which, he goes to church, THEN he comes here!" states Jack.

"I know. I just like to hear the way you tell it" States Willie. "And I just enjoy annoying the hell out of you. You need to come up for some air and get your face out of that computer screen." Everyone in the group roars with laughter.

Chapter 9 *Time for the police to arrive...*

Phillip joined the Boston Police department right out of college. He was surprised he passed the examination and oral interview, and was chosen to become one of Boston's Finest. But he always wanted to be a police officer, ever since he can remember. He dreamed of being a police detective, and driving around in an unmarked car wearing a suit, instead of a uniform.

He wondered would he work in Burglary, or Homicide? Perhaps he might land in the tactical unit, or the SWAT team. He had visions of grandeur for his future career. It all might have happened, had it not been for his debilitating injury, forcing his early retirement after only fourteen years on the job.

After graduating from the academy, he was assigned foot patrol directing traffic in the downtown area. But he wanted more excitement. He heard that the department was forming a special squad who would fight crime in streets downtown. Unfortunately, instead of a patrol car, he was assigned a patrol bicycle. It had all of the equipment he would need, and he would work with a partner. He didn't mind though. In fact he thought it made good sense.

The downtown area was congested with traffic. The bike would allow him to move around more freely. In a patrol car he be stuck in traffic all of the time. He was good at it to. On one occasion, a call came in about a bank robbery in one of the downtown branches. It only took a minute or so to get there. He learned that the robber had fled on foot. He got a good description and him and his partner were on their way in hot pursuit.

A short time later they spied an individual fitting the description in an alley across from City Hall. Splitting up they closed off the alley on each end. Phillip wheeled down the alley after the man. By this time additional backup had arrived and patrol cars were at each end. As the man ran, getting closer to the police car, he suddenly jumped over the hood, followed quickly behind by Phillip who leaped off of his bike and caught up to the guy with a flying tackle.

He wasn't hurt though, but the criminal sure was feeling the brunt of Phillip's six foot, two hundred and thirty pound frame landing across his back. They carted the crook off in an ambulance. All the money was recovered, and Phillip received his first, of many citations.

About six years later Phillip and his partner were chasing a man on a bike. It seems this guy had just snatched a purse from a lady walking across the street. As he and his partner quickly went after the man, the partner drove to the other side of the street.

So here were the two bike cops, riding parallel, on each side of the street, chasing after the man. Philip had his eyes trained on the guy, when someone tried to exit their parked car as the cop approached, not seeing him come. They flew open the driver's door and blocked Phillip's path. Phillip's bicycle hit the door full speed and he went flying forward in the air, landing on his shoulder first, and then flat on his back.

His partner ended the pursuit to attended to his friend. He called for an ambulance, and Phillip was carted off to the hospital in serious condition. He received a broken his shoulder, fracture to his leg and three broken vertebrae in his back. He's been off of work for the last five years, and is still going to therapy to ease the pain. Phillip is the baby in the group. He's in his early forties, but other folks his age are working, and not on disability like him. So he meets up with retired cops, and other folks.

As Phillip enters the shop he looks over at the group, smiles and nods his head Hi. At the same time he waves his hand into the air to everyone, but winces in pain, from the sore shoulder and back. He walks to the counter placing his order, then slowly proceeds to Smitty's table, and sits down. Smitty and Phillip enter into inaudible conversation.

When Cops get together, everything is secretive about their conversations. They still act like they're on the job. But they are basically two nice guys, who would give you the shirt off their backs. Well maybe not Smitty, he'd try to sell it to you.

O'Brien is another retired cop that come in frequently when he's not in Florida or the hospital. He's always smiling, and always has his digital camera with him. He's had two heart attacks, multiple pacemakers installed, etc. He's not in the best of health, but is always smiling.

His ailments do not interfere with his optimistic outlook on life. He enjoys his family and friends. He does walk kind of slow though, and rides his bicycle to the shop occasionally though, when there is good weather. He keeps himself very busy with a daily diary on his web Blog. He also loves his web email account.

He likes to read everything, and he also is notorious for forwarding everything that's sent to him. His presence on Facebook is astonishing to the younger generation in his family. But his mind is sharp as a tack, and he never argues.

His main affliction is for the young ladies. If he sees a cute one, he takes their picture. When he was on the force he worked Homicide. One of his jobs was to take the crime scene photos. So I guess it's in his blood to incessantly be working the camera. Only now he can take pleasant pictures, to wipe out all the gruesome recollections of the ones he's taken in the past.

As he walks into the shop he has his camera at the ready, draped around his neck with a string. He walks over to the group, and while on the way there, he snaps a picture.

"Hi Guys thought I'd take a picture of the group for my Blog. Hey, did I show you my pacemaker scars?"

As he starts to unbutton his shirt, he then notices the clerk, Nancy, behind the counter. He stops the unbuttoning, and turns back to the group. "Hey, she's new! And pretty too!" he states as he turns back to face the clerk. He slowly walks over to her, with a sheepish grin. " Mind if I get a picture?" he says.

"Whatever floats your boat, honey?"

He quickly snaps a few photos. "I'll have to put these on my Blog to show my friends in Florida." "Hey I see you've got some new items in the display case." He exclaims. "Let me get a picture." He walks up and down the front of counter, snapping away. Jack looks up from his computer. "What are you doing, O'Brien? Leave the girl alone."

"You know, got to have something to put on my BLOG! I thought I'd let the folks in Florida know what's new here in the shop."

"You mean new menu items, right, because the clerk IS NOT on the menu. Besides don't you think they have the same things in the shop in Florida? It is a chain you know!" states Jack

"Hey that's right, I didn't think of that. But that shop doesn't have all of you guys! Besides, OUR clerks are much prettier here in this shop! I think I'll put some photos on Facebook, and send them out in my email too. Just so I don't miss anyone."

Everyone looks at each other and roll their eyes. O'Brien puts his camera in his pocket and goes back to the counter to place his order.

"You know O'Brien. I was just thinking. All those pictures you take are the only things you've ever shot, in your entire career." States Phillip from the back table.

"HA, HA, HA, very funny. I've shot a lot of things in my career."

"I mean with a gun!" retorts Phillip.

"Ya, ya, ya, yada, yada, yada. At least, I didn't fall off of my tricycle, young man!"

"Ouuuuuuu" says the group.

Phillip looks annoyed and does not continue the conversation, but instead continues his talk with Smitty, while looking the other way.

Chapter 10   *Anybody need a ticket?*

In his younger days Robby was a truck driver by trade, tall and slender, in his sixties, but not fully retired. He's half Jewish on his mother's side, but does not really appreciate jokes about Jews. But sometimes members of the group forget that.

Some of them in the group seem to think that when they're telling their jokes, or making their off color humorous remarks, that they're only talking to his Christian side, because the Jew in him didn't come in shop that day. But he never says a word about it.

Right now his job is as a Community Service officer in one of the northern suburbs. He always comes into the shop wearing his uniform, which is white a police shirt, gabardine shorts and police hat. The other complimentary items are his short shorts, and over the ankle boots. He always wears the shorts. Whether it is summer or winter, he doesn't seem to mind the cold.

He is presently assigned in town to give out the parking violations on the meters. For this he gets to drive a four-wheeler ATV around town, chalk the tires, and give out the parking tickets. He seems to enjoy it, but is looking at retiring soon and relaxing.

He walked over to the counter and placed his order, then walked back to the table area. He spots a vacant seat, and sets his food down on the table. "Morning everyone!"

The group is starting to get pretty large now. They're all looking at him, and in unison they say "Hi Robby!"

"Morning guys!" Robby takes his cup and goes over to the coffee station to prepare his morning java. He then walks back to the table and sits down. "So, what's new with you guys?"

Well Robby, we're all wondering why Rick is so late. We're wondering why we haven't seen Louie in a while. We're wondering why O'Brien is so happy, and we're wondering why Smitty let the Homeless guy get away with is Danish?" States Jack.

"Homeless guy get away? What are you talking about?"

"Never mind, it's a long story, but someone came in and stole Smitty's Danish, and I might add he got away before Smitty realized it was taken. He must be slipping!" Jack reiterated.

"What kind of Danish was it?" Asks Robby in a naïve but sarcastic tone. Together the group laughs, as Jack chides. "Look, we got three cops in here right now. Smitty the patrolman; Phillip the Bicycle Cop; and O'Brien the Homicide Detective. I'm sure before we leave here today; they will have solved the crime. Smitty has been looking at his empty plate all morning in hopes of getting fingerprints or DNA. O'Brien is going to snap all the pictures they need of the crime scene, and Phillip is going to patrol the area looking for a shopping cart with a homeless man attached to it later. Perhaps you'd like to join them. Better yet, we could all form a posse and go out and look for the guy. I just wish ABBY were here from NCIS to help with the forensics. She's much better to look at then you old farts."

Just then Rick walks into the shop. He's not his usual self. He walks over to the tables and reaches into his pocket and pulls out a hundred dollar bill and holds it up for all to see. Rick is very somber as he speaks. "Guess what?" He holds out the bill in outstretched arms, and circles around the room in exaggeration.

"Louie?" Jack asks sadly.

"Yep, Happened last night."

"How'd you find out about it, what happened?" asks O'Brien.

"Well I was supposed to pick him up last night, and we were going out to eat and watch the game at the bar. As usual, he left his condo door unlocked, like he always does for me to get in. I opened the door and called out his name as I entered, but got nothing back. I went in and looked around and there he was, sitting on his couch in front of his big TV and there was a movie on. Immediately, I called 911, but it was too late. The Wake is Monday at O'Grady's."

"What movie was it?" snickers Robby.

The group did not think that was funny, as they had just lost another prominent member. They all gave Robby a disapproving stare. "Oh come on. You all know he'd think it was funny. After all who was it that pinned a hundred dollar bill to his bed, HIM, and always joked about it?" Robby states with empathy.

"Yes you're probably correct." States Phillip "So Rick, let me get this straight? You walk in and discover the body, and then you called 911?" He adds.

"That's right."

"Then you went in and got the hundred?" Smitty asks.

"Well not quite in that order. You see I wanted to get the hundred off of the bed before the Paramedics and Police came in, you know, so it didn't "disappear". So I went in and got that first; then I called 911. That's what he wanted me (or you if you found him) to do. But this money's not for me alone, he always said to treat all of you guys with it. So today, coffee is on Louie."

"So, why didn't you get here earlier, before we all had our coffee bought and paid for?" again asks Smitty

"Well, I had something to do at home first."

"Yes, we heard. Va Va Voom!" Chides Smitty with a hand gesture.

The entire group laughs for a moment, but then they change their mood and become silent. This changes to sadness and they remain quiet, but one by one they get up and get their coffee. When they get back to the table they raise their cups to each other.

In unison they state "TO LOUIE!"

Surprisingly all of the customers in the shop were paying attention to this announcement also. They too shout a reply "TO LOUIE!"

Chapter 11   *Let's go to the Mexican Riviera...*

At home he wakes up each morning and turns on the TV to catch the morning news. Once he is done grooming himself he trots on downstairs to the kitchen and to get some breakfast. He won't cook anything, but instead will have some cold cereal and juice.

He looks in the cabinets for some fresh coffee to make a pot, but there is none. He knows that if he doesn't have his morning coffee he'll start getting caffeine withdrawal, and a headache will ensue. So he'll have to go out and get some at the coffee shop.

Some think his money came from organized crime. Others think he was in sales, and still others think he owned his own business. Truth be told, his money came from investments, but these were not investments he made, instead they were investments he inherited.

Basically his is a pretty frugal spender when it comes to the normal things. He always looks for the deals, and the ways to avoid paying for them.

One time when the electric company had received permission from the Public Utility Commission to raise rates, he was outraged. So outraged that he called them up to complain, but to no avail. So his next call was to his broker. Where he bought a large amount of utility stock.

His thinking was that since the utility stock was paying four-dollar dividend, he'd buy enough stock that the dividends received would be enough to pay for the utility bill. This way he'd never have to pay another one again.

He drove a new top of the line BMW and made sure he parked it in areas away from the other cars, so it wouldn't get scratched or nicked. He thought about trying to get a handicap-parking permit, but his conscious wouldn't let him do it. So for now, he'll just have to endure the long walks to the stores entrances.

His given name was Anthony, but he was known around the coffee shop as Mexican Toni. He was tall, fit and trim and always wore a gold chain around his neck, complimented by a large fake Rolex watch on his wrist. There was no way he was going to pay for a real one if he didn't have too.

Now, he's not called Mexican Toni because he is Mexican, but because he always is going to Mexico on holidays and vacations. He always lets everyone know how much he pays for these trips, which are far more, than anyone would ever pay for a trip. Which alone goes against his character. But he wants the best of the best when he travels and spares no expense. He'll not shop around for these things, because he can't be bothered to invest the time.

Today he enters the shop wearing a black satin jacket, dark sunglasses, slacks and black dress shoes. His hair is slicked back and neatly coiffed into a ponytail in the back. His skin is always tanned and he walks with a sense of pride. "Hi Guys!"

"Hey Toni, haven't seen you in a while! Been in Mexico again?" asks Robby.

While the men are talking a pretty young lady walks into the shop and approaches the counter. She glances over at the group of old men when Rick notices her looking. "Hi, How ya doing, Good to see ya." He states. She turned away and continued with the clerk, not saying anything in return. Rick fees rejected. He cannot understand why she did not acknowledge his greeting. "Whoa Boy!" he states.

"Just got back from Puerto Viallarta. Spent the weekend there paid six thousand dollars for my wife and me for a week. Had a great time."

"Yes, but we mean, we haven't seen you in a long, long, time." States Jack.

"Well before that, it was Guarda LaHara, spent eight thousand on that one and before that did a Mexican Riviera cruise. That one cost twelve thousand."

Jack starts putting his computer away, as does Smitty. Jack gets up and puts on his coat. "Leaving Jack?" Asks Rick.

"Yes, gotta go." Jack looks at Rick and smiles as he sarcastically states. "I'm going to go home and plan my next trip. Choose a good campground. You know I'm looking at one that cost three hundred a night. More amenities than a Marriott!" Toni looks at Jack with displeasure.

"I'm leaving too." Says Smitty. "Me too." Said Phillip

"Same here, but I'll be in the back. My wife's in here now, and I'm going to sit with the girls, you know, her and her friends." Said O'Brien.

"Well I'm not sticking around either I just stopped in to get my coffee, and to say hi."

By this time everyone else gets up and they all put on their coats, except Rick, who sits quietly. "Let me know what time the wake is for Louie, and what day you're going, will you?" states Jack.

"I will, I'll call you."

As the men leave one by one, Rick is the only one left in the group. He looks around and sees no one in the shop that is familiar to him. So he goes back to reading his newspaper. It's now 11:30 AM and he'll also have to leave soon, but for now he changes the page on his newspaper, and while holding it up in front of him he states. "Whoa Boy!" and the room goes silent except for the music in the background.

Chapter 12   *The group is dwindling...*

It's now five years later, and many things have happened to members of this group during that time. The remaining members are attending the wake of the most recent member to pass on. They are gathering in the viewing area at O'Grady's funeral home. This is an old family funeral parlor run by Irish immigrants who came to the Boston area in the 1850's.

The outside resembles a large granite, two-story mansion, with a high stairway from the street level to the entrance door. The windows on the corner of the building have curved glass, and the transom over the double entrance door has a leaded glass design in it.

Upon entering there is a large staircase just inside and on the left. The hallway to the right has a doorway directly adjacent to the entrance door, and a second one shortly down the hallway. There is deep red wallpaper with a large leaf pattern on it, complimented by red Persian rugs with another green leaf pattern.

Hanging from the ceiling is a large crystal chandelier. A short way up from the floor is a painted white enamel molding that runs along the entire hallway meeting up against the trim around the doorframes.

Upon entering the viewing room one would see a similar architecture, with large crown molding at the ceiling. Since there is a large turnout expected for this way, the room divider between the two rooms has been folded back for a larger area to expose itself and allow for additional seating.

The casket is in the front of the room and directly in front it is a kneeler of dark oak with a black velvet cushion to kneel on. Set back from that and directly in front of the viewer's chairs is an antique divan for the family to use.

The casket itself is made of mahogany and is highly polished. The handles on each side of it are made of pewter. At the head and foot of it, are two tall and lit pewter candles. The bed linens inside are of a pale quilted yellow satin. Its resident lays there, dressed in a dark blue suit, white shirt, and patterned yellow tie. His hands are neatly folded and a rosary is interlaced in between his fingers. He looks peaceful.

On either side of the casket there are flower sprays of white daisies. The one on the left says "Dad" while the one on the right says "Husband". There is a small table way to the left that contains many family photos on a large poster board, and an open box of his favorite chocolates, Turtles for the people who come.

Also there is a newspaper, and his laptop is opened up and plugged in. There is a slide show being played with additional photos of him or his favorite things. He insisted they be there for his friends to see and candy to take. I'm sure by now your wondering who it is? Whose wake they are all attending? Well there is a third flower spray. It has blue violets, and white roses. The banner is red and flows diagonally from top to bottom. On it in gold letters is the word "JACK"

His children were present, and his wife was in the lounge when some of the men arrive. Rick is already in the room and standing in front of the casket. He is quiet and his head is hung low. The remaining members of the group enter the room. Smitty, Phillip, Stu, and two new members, who recently started coming to the coffee shop. Their names are Cliff and Stan. They are also elderly, with Cliff being about ten years younger than Stan. Stan's hair is white, while Cliffs is just graying on the sides. Stan uses a walker to get around.

They are standing off to the side talking to one another waiting for the people in front of the casket to clear. Stan walks over to the seating area and takes a chair with the walker in front of him, while Cliff patiently is standing next to him. Smitty now enters the room and sees Rick in front of the casket. Smitty walks over and stands beside Rick, placing his hand on his shoulder. At this time Cliff and Stan are to the side talking to each other.

Stu enters the room and looks at the casket, then looks around the room and spies the table display. He walks over to where it is set up against the wall gazing at the layout of the items. On the table is a newspaper. Stu picks up the paper and walks back to a chair, but then turns back quickly, and grabs a piece of candy, and sits down by himself. Stu begins to read the paper.

"Well, it was just a matter of time, overweight, and he didn't take his health seriously. It's too bad. He was only 67. He just started collecting his social security last year." Rick states to Smitty.

"Yes, but because of his age, and the economy, he never did get a job, and with his social security? Well, it wasn't enough to pay for his meds, so he just stopped taking them. You know he had that COPD crap, you know, what do they call it? Oh ya, Chronic Obstructive Pulmonary Disease. His meds alone cost two hundred and fifty dollars per month." Stated Smitty.

"Yes, and he had sleep apnea too." Replies Rick.

"It's so sad. Us old farts need more and more meds to just stay alive. When you think about it, five years ago there were so many of us at the shop on the weekends. We'd meet, we'd talk, and we'd laugh. We had good times on those weekend mornings. But you know it would look more like him if they got rid of the rosary and put his notebook in his hands. He was never without it" Exclaims Smitty.

"I know, remember when Louie died, and shortly after that O'Brien? Then there was the tragic death of Dr. Doom. After that came Green Lake Willie; Mexican Toni; Nicky, and now Jack. Who's next? It's been a crappy last five years. There are not many of us left. Seems like as soon as one leaves group, then someone else joins. Like Cliff and Stan."

"Hey, over the years our friends come and go. All you can do is remember the good times we had with them, and continue on. We can't live forever. Our group is not unique. Members enter and leave. You can go anywhere and find similar groups of old people, all over. The older we get, the more frequently death happens. I'm just getting tired of funerals." Said Smitty.

"I know what you mean. But you know, it's kind of funny, how old men find each other. Weather it's in our coffee shop, or at the mall, they seek each other out. They overcome their prejudices, and find commonalities, or just tolerate each other because they're all in the same boat. I guess getting old can bring out the best in you." Said Rick.

As Rick speaks Smitty is constantly nodding in agreement. He rubs his hand in a comforting gesture across Rick's back and says. "Come on; let's go over by Cliff and Stan. I have no idea what Stu is up to. Lay a paper down, and he's sure to grab it!"

"Jacks wife put it there. It was one of the things he wanted on the table. He knew his friend Stu would show up, and being kind of quiet, he wanted him to be himself." Stated Rick

Both men walk over to Cliff and Stan, who stop their conversation and look up at the men approaching. However, Rick and Smitty have both aged, and their walk is somewhat labored. When they reach them, they engage in small talk. "I did not know him that well," stated Stan. "Neither did I" stated Cliff. "Well you should have started coming by the shop a long time ago. He was quite a character. But always loyal to his friends." Said Rick. "It was in the last year or so his health took a dramatic downward spiral." Said Smitty.

Inaudible conversation ensues amongst the men when Robby walks into the room. He walks into the parlor, looks around while walking over to the casket. He stands there in front of it and is silent. Stu gets up from his seat and puts his paper down. He walks up to Robby and stands next to him.

"Kind of creepy seeing him lay there. Where's his wife, I want to give her my condolences." Robby said.

"She is downstairs in the coffee room with some of the other relatives. You know what she did?"

"No what" said Robby

"She had the coffee shop supply the coffee and pastries for all of the guests."

"No kidding!" exclaimed Robby. "He was like a fixture in the coffee shop." He continued.

"I know, and before him was that guy Fred, but he moved away. Fred has never come back to the shop, even to visit. Don't even know if he's alive any more. Then there was that old guy they called the Captain. Retired, Navy man, from WWII. He used to wear the same suit all the time, but he passed away a while ago. He couldn't wait to tell you about the war, what a character" stated Robby.

"I don't think I ever met Fred. He must have been before I started going there. I do remember the Captain though. All these old guys had so many stories to tell," said Stu.

"I know. The sad part is that once they go, their stories are lost forever. Some of these guys were real characters, real hero's, they actually made a mark on history in some way shape or form, and now their contributions will be lost forever" repeated Robby

"But for every one of us that goes, another one comes in. And life goes on. Let's go over by Rick and Smitty"

"OK" replied Robby. Both men leave and walk over to where the rest of the group is. They stand around in a small circle chatting with each other. The funeral is held the next day, and following that the men in the group are back at the coffee shop.

Chapter 13   *Getting back into the routine...*

The day is Saturday and it is a week after Jack's funeral. The old men have had time to adjust to the resizing of the group. Psychologically they all know that there will be new members joining their unofficial organization. They slip into their normal daily activities, but all are intent on meeting up at the coffee shop today and on the future weekends.

Inside the coffee shop the clerk behind the counter is busy preparing her cash register draw. The time is 5:45 AM and the shop is not officially open yet, but the doors are unlocked. Rick is the first to arrive, and enters the shop. He has his newspaper tucked under his arm. It is summer, and he does not have on a coat. He is wearing a short sleeve dress shirt and dress slacks. It's the same old

Rick, just a few years older, and moving slightly slower.

"Good morning sir. I'm not officially open, but the coffee is ready, and I'll give you a cup to get some. You can pay me later."

Rick does not recognize this clerk. She is new. He thinks to himself that she will not be able to serve him as efficient and he'll have to train her. He really doesn't understand, that it will be the other way around. Her name is Ashley and she is about 24 years old. She transferred in from another store, and is well versed in what her duties are and how to take care of her customers. She reaches under the counter and hands one of the small cups to Rick.

"Small one right?" she says.

Rick looks astonished that she knew how to fill his order. He states.

"How'd you know how to fill that order?"

"Well young man you have quite a reputation. We take pride in knowing all about our regular customers. In fact we have photos and profiles on the wall in the back of our best and most loyal ones"

"You do!" exclaims Rick loudly.

"No, I'm just kidding, the manager told me you'd probably be the first on in and what to expect. We're not THAT good!"

"Wow, I'm impressed. Your going to be a lot of fun, and you'll fit right in with this crowd."

"But I don't have any exact change right now, my registers not open yet, can you come back later to pay you when you're ready to leave." Said Ashley

"That's perfectly OK. I'll get you later."

Rick walks over to his usual table and puts down his paper. He takes his cup and walks over to the coffee station and pours his coffee. He walks back to the table and places the cup down. Then walks over to the water cooler and takes a plastic cup and pours his usual glass of Ice Water and walks back to the table and places it down. Just as he is about to take his seat a young lady walks in and goes up to the counter. She glances over at Rick. Rick interrupts his sitting and stands back up. "Hi! How you doing? Good to see you."

The woman acknowledges Rick with a small smile and nod. Rick continues to sit down. He takes his paper, and holding it with both hands, stretches it out and gives it a quick shake to remove the wrinkles while stating "Whoa Boy!"

A short while later Cliff and Stan enter the shop together. Cliff is dressed in a sweater and slacks and dress shoes but is not wearing socks. Stan is wearing a t-shirt with a leather vest over it. He has his walker and limps as he is walking. Stan and Cliff are very close friends, and choose a table close to Rick's. Stan sits down while Cliff stands next to the table.

"Good morning Rick!" states Cliff

"Ya, 'morning Rick!" adds Stan

Rick looks up from his paper and down at Cliff's shoes.

"Oh hi guys! I didn't see you guys come in. I guess I was too busy reading my paper. Hey Cliff! No socks?" Rick asks.

"I can't stand SOCKS in the summer. Whether they're on my feet or on the playing field. I hate the socks!" Cliff says. He pauses for a moment and looks to his partner. "OK Stan, what do you want?"

"Just coffee. Just get the cup, Ill get the coffee myself."

"No, you just sit there. I'll get it for you" replies Cliff as he walks over to the counter to place his order.

"Good morning sir, what can I get for you?" states Ashley in a chipper friendly tone.

"Just two small coffees please."

"Why certainly sir, that will be three seventy-four." She states.

Cliff reaches into his pocket to get his wallet. He reaches inside of it, and takes out a five-dollar bill and hands it to the clerk. "Keep the change."

"I'm sorry sir, but we can't take tips from customers. Here is your change, but thanks for offering it though?"

Cliff walks back to the table and hands one of the cups to Stan. Stan starts to get up to walk over to the coffee station to fill his cup. Cliff motions with his hand for him to sit back down. Another woman of middle age walks into the shop. She glances over to the old men, as she walks to the counter. "Hi! How are you doing? Good to see ya."

The woman glances over towards Rick and nods when Cliff speaks to Stan. "Stan, I told you to just sit there, I'll get your coffee!" Rick redirects his attention towards Stan. When he hears Stan speaking. He notices Stan's limp. "What happened to you, you were fine yesterday? I mean I know you use a walker, but you're walking much worse than when I saw you last."

"Slipped in the tub taking a shower. Now I need to get a grab bar installed. Just a small sprain, it's a bitch to get old."

"You live alone don't you?" asks Rick.

"Yes, my wife died about three years ago. Kids all live away. If it weren't for my good friend Cliff, I wouldn't have any help at all, you know, with the routine stuff. I help him, and he helps me. You know, we old geezers got to stick together." As Stan finishes speaking Cliff comes back to the table and sits down. He hands Stan his coffee.

"I tried to talk him into selling his house, and moving into one of those assisted living places, but he wants no part of It." states Cliff.

"I'm not giving up my freedom to those people. You go there, and then a few months later, they move you to the next floor level, where you're no different than being in a nursing home. The higher the floor, the worse off you are, both physically and mentally. Then, the next level is a trip to the happy hunting grounds. Nope, it's not for me. When I go it'll be in my own home," exclaims Stan.

"Ya, and I'll probably be the one to find you. I think you should pin a hundred dollar bill to the bedspread like Louie did, at least it would be worth my while" laughs Cliff

"Boy, I haven't thought about him in years. He was a character though. Kind of miss his big shit-eating grin when he used to walk in here," states Rick

Smitty now walks into the shop. He has his computer briefcase slung over his shoulder. He's wearing a t-shirt with big NRA logo on it. The bulge from his gun is visible underneath. He hobbles over to the table where Rick is sitting, and places his computer case on the vacant chair. His limp is on the same side he carries his gun on. "Morning Smitty" states Rick.

"Morning Rick! Hey how bout those Red Sox last night huh?" Smitty retorts.

"Yeah quite a game" replies Rick as Smitty hobbles over to the counter and is greeted by Ashley.

"Good morning sir!" Ashley says cheerfully.

"Coffee and a Danish please."

"Why certainly sir. That'll be two ninety-eight." She replies.

Smitty reaches for his wallet, but comes up empty. He searches all of his pockets but cannot find his wallet. He hobbles over to Rick's table, embarrassed and addresses Rick. "Hey Rick, I hate to ask this but could you give me five dollars. I seemed to have left my wallet at home." Rick has a big grin on his face as he reaches for his wallet. "You know what's funny about this?"

"How about.......... Nothing!" said Smitty.

"No there really is!" replies Rick.

"What then?"

Rick begins, "Well you forgot your wallet. BUT...you didn't forget your gun, or your computer! I guess we know where your priorities are. Gun first, computer, second, and wallet third. Oh ya, then there's the car keys, in that order. And you always use a credit card. You're going to have to go to the bank to get the five dollars and pay me back."

"HA HA. ...Just give me the five...PLEASE!" begs Smitty.

"Here. But if you weren't carrying the gun all those years you'd be in better shape. Instead of being lop-sided."

"How's that" asks Smitty?

"The limp you have isn't because you're so old, but because the gun is so heavy it's weighing you down. The limp is not from something physical ailment. It looks like your carrying a cannon in your pants" quickly chides Rick

Smitty looks back with a sinister smile. "That's not a cannon in my pants that's weighing me down."

"Well we all know it's certainly not your wallet!"

Smitty replies with an annoying laughter, "HA, HA, HA!"

The group breaks out in laughter while Rick stands up and removes his belt. He stretches it out on the table and starts to unzip a zipper that is on the underside. He reaches inside, and removed a small folded bill. It is a five and is folded very small, and tucked away in a secret compartment of the belt. He unfolds it and stretches it out on the table smoothing it out to remove the wrinkles and then gingerly hands it to Smitty, and then puts the belt back on.

"Whew, when you got up, I thought you were going to take your pants off. I didn't need the coffee that bad. But I should've known you'd be carrying around your life savings with you somewhere, I just couldn't imagine where. But thanks for the loan.

Smitty walks back over to the counter and hands the clerk the five-dollar bill. He gets his tray and cup, and walks over to the coffee station to fill it. After walking back over to Rick's table, he sits down. This is the seat that was always occupied by Jack. Smitty takes his computer out of its case and fires it up. He's now ready for whatever is thrown his way.

"So Rick. What was the score of last night's game?" asks Cliff.

"I don't know. It was a late game and I fell asleep in my easy chair. There's no sports section in my paper. It only has business news. Hey Smitty, look it up!"

Chapter 14   *Let's make some money…*

There is momentary silence as a tall trim gentleman enters the shop. His name is Ari and he is originally from the USSR. When Ari was a child he lived in the Ukraine, which was under communist rule at that time. His parents immigrated to the United States shortly after World War II. He grew up here in the US in the fifties and sixties during the cold war. Ari speaks fluent Russian and English.

During his high school years, he attended a military academy in Indiana, and then went to Notre Dame for college. He majored in Finance and Economics and, after graduating he took a position with a large brokerage firm in Chicago. While working there, he attended night school at the University of Chicago, and received his MBA in International Finance.

He successfully worked his way up the corporate ladder, during which he changed employers a few times. He was very successful. His financial and career success enabled him to purchase a seat on the Commodities Exchange. There he enjoyed much investing success, and was fortunate enough to be able to sell this seat in the seven figure range, and retire at a very young age.

Today he is 60 years old. He practices his religion as an Eastern Orthodox Catholic. He catches up with the group at the coffee shop on weekends after church services. He amuses himself with these visits. He likes to hear the amateurs discuss the market activities and hear what some of the old men are investing in. He laughs to himself when he hears their latest stock tip, because he knows that by the time these men here the news it is already old and too late to take advantage of.

While he traded, his philosophy was, if the price of the item would raise four cents a share, it was time to sell. By not being greedy enabled his success. However, when he bought and sold, it was in the millions of shares, not the small share volumes that these guys trade in. He does lend a hand though in explaining the different symbols, how the market works, and types of funds.

He has been here in the United States for many years now and has very strong opinions when it comes to business, investing, and his politics. Outside of the shop he is a very private man. He enjoys boating and has a large yacht in on the Cape in one of the harbors. His solace is going to his boat, which he uses frequently, and just relaxing at dockside in the summer. Cocktail in hand, and a newspaper at his side.

Rick is always happy to see him when he comes in, because he likes to pick his brain for advice on the market. Air enjoys this knowledge exchange with Rick who has a financial understanding better than the rest of the group, as well as he has the funds to bring the advice to fruition.

Ari is a very fashionable dresser. Today he is wearing a Ralph Lauren bright yellow polo shirt. Above the breast pocket there is an embroidered logo that says Boston Commercial Club. He compliments this with white Tommy Bahama dress shorts and Rockport boat shoes. His Burberry sweater is draped over his shoulders, with the sleeves half tied around his neck.

Ari walks to the counter and orders a cup of coffee, pays for it, and walks back over to the tables where the men are all sitting. He grabs an empty seat and sits down stirring his coffee, as he listens attentively to the conversation at hand.

"Morning Ari! You look like your going somewhere today?" states Rick.

"Yes I am. We had my grand daughter for a sleepover last night, and we're taking her to my boat for a short cruise on the lake. We'll stop in Salem at Pickering Warf for lunch. Then, we're going back to my daughters in Beverly to drop her off. She's going to meet us at the harbor wharf, so I can't stay here long. It's going to be a long day. I just hope the winds are down and the weather holds steady."

"Oh Ari! By the way, this is Cliff and this is Stan. They just started coming here a few weeks ago." Both Cliff and Stan rise and extend their hands to Ari, but Stan is having trouble getting up, so Ari gets up from his seat and walks over to Stan to shake his hand. He then goes back to his seat and sits down.

"Glad to meet you." Ari states.

"So Ari, what do you think of the market right now?" asks Rick

"Well, it can't stay this way forever. Something has to give. I've got a big deal I 'm about to close on." Ari says this with a small smile on his face. He is baiting the men in the shop to ask more questions about his soon to be purchases in the market.

"What is it? Can I get in on it?" asks Rick excitedly. Rick is fidgeting in his chair in excitement. He leans forward to Ari as he speaks. The other men also lean in Ari's direction so they do not miss out on a single word.

Ari pauses and looks around the shop before speaking. He notices that there are people at the counter, and other patrons throughout the shop who are busy in their own conversations. He looks back at Rick. " Sure if you want to, but listen carefully, because I don't want any misunderstandings if you screw it up. You're on your own with this investment. After I tell you, I have nothing to do with it and no responsibility for it OK?"

Rick is watering at the mouth by now. He can't wait to hear what this hot tip is. He's already counting his profits in his head. "OK, just tell us will you!" Rick says with excitement. Ari begins to speak. "Well, I'm putting my money..." As Ari speaks, the entire shop goes quiet, and all the patrons listen attentively.

Heads are turning at the other tables, newspapers are being put down, and the clerks behind the counter stop what they're doing. The entire place is quiet now. Ari notices this, and glances around, with a big grin on his face and turns back to Rick.

"In GUMBALLS!" he states.

"GUMBALLS?" Rick replies with astonishment, as Ari laughs out loud.

Laughing now uncontrollably, Ari replies with a chuckle in his voice. "Yes, that's' right, Gumballs. They cost less than a penny to make and they sell for a quarter. That's a twenty-five hundred percent profit margin. You know there's even a Gumball mutual fund. The fund manager will invest in all the different colors, shapes and sizes. You know, Wrigley, Trident, Bazooka, and Double Bubble. You should get in on it."

Rick does not know whether to take him seriously or whether he is pulling his leg. "What's the symbol?" asks Rick.

Ari holds up his hand and makes the symbol "O" with his thumb and forefinger while trying to hold back his laughter he states at the same time. "O"

Rick looks over to Smitty. He does not have to say anything because Smitty can anticipate what's coming next and states. "I know, Smitty, look it up!" Ari notices that others in the room are listening and writing down the information he has divulged. He chuckles to himself while stating to the group. "You guys are so gullible. You come in here, day after day, and anything that someone says you take it to be a good tip. You can't get good advice on investing in the stock market, in a coffee shop."

"Yes, I should have known you were kidding. Now that you mention it, coffee shop tips are what got Green Lake Willie, Nicky, and Dr. Doom into trouble" states Rick.

"Don't forget that! It's the best piece of advice that I could ever give you guys. Well, I've got to go now. See you all later. Nice to meet you Cliff, and you too Stan."

Cliff and Stan start to rise and get their stuff together to leave, and Smitty starts to pack up his stuff but stops, and sit back down.

Just then a young lady walks into the shop. She glances over at the group as they shuffle their things in their preparation to leave. Rick, as usual notices her immediately as she approaches the counter. "Hi! How ya doing, good to see ya?" She nods, and gives a small smile, then looks back at the counter and away from the men.

Cliff and Stan sit back down to watch her. Ari gets up, grabs his coffee and leaves the shop. The men go back to their preparations to leave, while Rick looks at Ari as he walks out the door. He then focuses back to his paper. He picks up the paper and stretches it out.

"Whoa boy!"

Another woman enters the shop. She is dressed in spiked high heels and tight jeans. All of the men look her over. Rick notices her and puts his paper down on the table. She glances over at the remaining men, and then at Rick. "Hi! How ya doing, good to see ya?" he says.

"Man those heels are tall! I wonder what the highest heels are?" states Stan.

"Hey Jack...I mean Smitty...look it up!" exclaims Rick

Smitty just smiles while he types on the keyboard quickly. Rick is so used to stating that command to Jack he forgot himself.

"Wow, I almost forgot, he's, I mean, Jack's not here. Funny how you take for granted the "regulars". like, they're a fixture in this place. They were always here, and always available for conversation." States Rick

Smitty finishes typing and looks up At Rick. "I know. It feels funny sitting here in this seat, instead of over there. But you and Jack always had the seats in the window."

"Yes there are so many of us that don't come in here anymore, or anywhere else for that matter, because they're all gone. They got old, or sick, or just simply passed away for one reason or another. But they all had their amusing anecdotes, stories, character flaws, personalities, and uniqueness; I guess we're just a bunch of interesting individuals." Rick states.

"Did I ever tell you guys about the time Nicky was going to square off with the big Irish guy?"

Rick continued as Smitty stops packing, while Stan and Cliff, sit back down. Together they say in unison. "NO!"

Just as Rick is about to tell the story Robby walks into the shop. He's wearing his uniform and has his usual shorts on. He walks directly to the counter without looking over at the group, places his order and pays for it.

"Hey Robby! Come on over you have to hear this one," yells Rick from across the room.

Robby grabs his items off of the counter and walks over to the coffee station where he fills up his cup. He then walks over to where the group is gathered, and puts his things down on an empty table, then sits to listen to Rick while greeting all in the group. "Morning guys, what's going on?"

"I was just about to tell these guys the story about Nicky and the Irish guy. You remember that guy that used to come in here years ago they called Nicky don't you?" asks Rick.

"Why of course I do. He used to come in here all of the time. That is until he went and died. Go ahead continue, don't let me hold you up?"

"OK. So here it is on a Sunday Morning. Nicky is sitting here with is wife, and Jack is sitting over there." Rick points to different areas of the room. "And this big Irish guy limps in. He had a bum leg." Rick get up from his chair and is exaggerating a limp, imitating what he observed. "Now you have to remember or keep in mind that Jack is 10 years, or so, younger than Nicky."

"So what happened?" Cliff states with excitement.

"First let me paint a picture for you about this guy. He, the Irish guy, came into the shop quite frequently. Now you remember when the coffee shop would put out free samples on a table over there?" Rick points over to the coffee station.

"Well, the Irish guy never bought anything. He'd just come in and take the samples. He'd put them in a napkin, and sit at an empty table. He'd compliment this meal with a glass of ice water he'd take from the back." Rick started as they all listened attentively.

"Whenever he talked, he had a thick accent, which sometimes made it difficult for people to understand what he was saying. Most of the time you just nodded. Anyway, he was about fifty years old, well over six feet tall, and was bald on the top on his head. He always came in wearing a big brown hat, and most always had on a raggedy old overcoat.

Rumor had it he lived right here in the downtown area in the basement of a building his ex-wife owned. They were divorced and he was just shy of being homeless. Anyway he started yelling across the room at Jack. We don't know if he was drunk or what. He starts asking Jack all kinds of personal questions. Like where he worked, how much money he made, where he lived, what kind of car he drove. Jack was visibly annoyed, because his answers were evasive and vague."

Rick continued "Jack would redirect his focus by engaging in conversation with Nicky hoping to avoid any further discussion with the Irish guy. Because of that, Jack ignoring him, the Irish guy was starting to get pissed off and asked Jack if he thought he was too good for him, to which Jack ignored him further. You could see the anger building up in the Irish guy."

"I can see why!" interjected Stan.

"So Nicky, all five foot six of him, tells this big Irish guy to shut up and stop with all the questions, and leave Jack alone, can't you see he doesn't want to talk to you, Nicky told the Irishman, to which the Irishman now started to argue with Nicky. The argument escalated louder and louder between the two men. The whole coffee shop became silent. The shop manager came out from the back to see what the commotion was all about."

"As the argument ensued, with each of them calling the other names, the two of them get up, right here in the window, and they're going to duke it out, when the manager finally steps in between them, and asks the Irish guy to leave, or he was going to call the police."

"So that's it, that's all that happens?" asks Stan.

"No, that's not all, let me continue. By now the Irish guy is really pissed. He knows if he continues he's going to jail, so he pauses, looks at everybody and walks out."

"Come on, that can't be all there is to it," interrupts Robby.

"I Told you, be patient, it gets a lot better."" Rick exclaims.

"Now when this guy left the shop, he went out the front door of the shop right there by that window." Rick points outside. "The Irishman walked over to a bicycle that was leaning up against that post over there. He grabbed the bicycle, mounted it, and driving quite wobbly, simply drove away?"

"So what?" says Stan.

"Well as it turns out, it seems the bicycle wasn't his to take. He just stole it, right in front of us. The patron who it belonged to didn't notice it until they were leaving. We told him what had happened, and who took it. Sometime later we read in the local newspaper that the Irishman was arrested for stealing bikes all over town, and selling them on Craig's list. He's now in jail, resting peacefully I might add, and getting his freebies there too, if you like a constant diet of boloney sandwiches."

"I guess Nicky was lucky nothing happened," said Robby

"Are you kidding me? The lucky one was the Irish guy. He didn't know that Nicky used to be a Golden Gloves boxer in his younger days, with 21 fights. His record was 20-0-1. He never went pro because he was too small. He would have killed the Irishman. You never know the real stories about the people who come in here. Some may be old, but they're tough as nails too."

Rick continues, "Another story is about the time Walden Pond Willie called one of the ladies stupid. Walden Pond passed away a while ago, but I'll tell you how that happened later."

"Who's the lady?" asks Cliff.

"Well she was this nice quiet gentle woman who used to come in here with her husband. She was intelligent and could keep a conversation going with all of us old geezers with no problem. They used to sit right over there." Rick points to a corner of the room away from the front windows.

"Anyway, one day while her husband was at the counter getting their order, she was telling us how she was applying for a job to be a census taker, and had to go online to take the test. She stated how difficult a process it was, because she was applying for a supervisory position. Willie listened to her, and after she gave examples of some of the questions she had to answer, he had the nerve to actually say to her that if she didn't know the answers to those questions, then she must be stupid."

"You're kidding. If he ever said that to my wife, he'd be hanging outside from the light pole," Smitty stated.

"I know we were all shocked when we heard it. I would do the same as you suggested if he said it to my wife. However, the lady's husband, upon hearing of this, just sat there, fuming. Now here is a guy in his late forties who is well over six feet tall, and more than two hundred and fifty pounds, while Willie is a shrimp of a man in his seventies. Anyway, even though he could of killed Willie, he patiently ate his food, drank his coffee, and shortly thereafter, the lady and her husband abruptly left.

After that incident when they came in, which is not that often, if Willie was here, they would sit in the back or just leave. When in fact Willie was the one that was really stupid. He was so stupid that he couldn't figure out why whenever he came into the shop, the folks in the group or other people just excused themselves, and one by one started to leave."

"I know. I used to do that. The funny thing about it was; he started to come in earlier and earlier. He thought the people were leaving because THEY had been there so long. One day he came in when the place first opened. He was the only one here. When the regulars came in or saw him from outside, they would either get back into their cars and leave, or simply ask the clerk for their coffee to go," said Robby.

"This place is so full of stories and anecdotes. I could go on forever, given enough time," stated Rick.

Chapter 15 *What happened to everybody...*

"Hey Rick, why don't you tell them how Willie died, it 's morbidly funny." Stated Robby.

"Well that's a story all in itself. It seems that one-day; over at the church when Willie and his cronies were counting the money, they had two money machines. One of them was used to count the paper bills, and the other one was a huge commercial one for counting the coins. Willie was busy at the coin counter."

Rick continued. "As he poured in the coins they jammed up in the chute. As the tumbler went round and round the coins were not processing properly, and it wasn't counting them right. So instead of turning off the machine like your supposed to, Willie stuck his hand down the chute to clear it. As he bent over, his tie flopped into the chute and started to wind up getting shorter and shorter.

No one could hear anything because of the loudness of the machine and the coin noise within it. So his tie was caught inside the coin counter. It kept spinning around and winding up his tie. He wrestled to get it loose but could not. None of his cronies were aware of his struggle and when the tie ran out of slack, it simply strangled him.

They finally saw him dangling there from the machine by his neck and cut the tie off, but it was too late. He was already dead, and the paramedics that were called could not revive him. Another funeral at O'Grady's"

"Go on, we've got some time, tell them about the rest of the guys" Smitty said.

"OK. How about the death of Dr. Doom? You see Dr. Doom liked to take these exercise walks after he left here. He was so vane about his looks. He dreaded getting old. Well he used to keep these thirty-pound dumbbells in his trunk. He would go to his car, take them out, and pump the iron up and down, just like Rocky in the movies, while he was walking. You could almost here the music playing as he walked by."

"Continue, I'm fascinated," Smitty says sarcastically.

"OK already! Well, one day he was doing this, walking down the street, and pumping the iron dumbbells up and down, a young lady pulled into a parking space near him, and was parking her car. She was in a red convertible and had the top down. Well, it seems that she had on a very revealing and short skirt, and when she exited the car, it was quite a site, distracting him.

It was such a distraction that while he was pumping to impress her with his virility, that he hit himself in the head with one of the dumbbells. This caused him to become slightly dizzy and he fell down backwards and cracked the back of his head on the curb. This blow to the back of the head was his demise." Rick pauses and ponders for a moment, then continues.

"Let's see now, Louie died in his apartment of a heart attack, and O'Brien, oh yeah O'Brien. That's another good one."

"Well lets hear it," asked Stan

"Well OK. You see once there were these two sisters who were twins and they used to come in here occasionally. I mean these girls were beautiful. They were also State Police officers. The were known collectively as the Waldron sisters. So here they are and they're in their uniforms. O'Brien got this idea. See he had a Pace Maker for his heart, and they were Peace Makers. So he decides he is going to get his picture taken with them and he is going to title it, The Pacemaker meets the Peacemakers.

So here he is standing between them with his arms around each one. Someone takes his camera, and snaps the picture. He goes home and he puts it on his Blog that night. This was his shining moment. To have his picture taken with these two beautiful women. The next morning he does not wake up. We could only conclude that he fulfilled his last wish, to be in the arms of two beautiful women, and he died with a smile on his face. This of course meant another trip over to O'Grady's."

"Let's see, Jack from COPD and obesity, the Captain of a heart attack, I told you about Willie, and Dr. Doom, who am I missing? Oh yes, Mexican Toni and Nicky!" Rick thinks another moment.

"Ok here goes. Well it seems that while Mexican Toni was on one of his infamous and expensive cruises; he didn't show up at bedtime. At first his wife thought this was odd, but Toni liked to sit in the lounge chairs up on the deck at night, and enjoy the cool breezes, so she wasn't too concerned at first.

The next morning his wife couldn't find him. She looked everywhere and finally talked to the ships security officer and told them about it. They searched the entire ship, top to bottom. He was nowhere to be found. They concluded he fell overboard. The conducted a sea search but came up with nothing. Sad part is his wife has to wait seven years to collect anything before the insurances would pay." Rick stated.

"Yes, or he was pushed because someone was tired of hearing all his bragging crap!" said Smitty

"And last but not least there's Nicky. Now, Nicky, that was another strange one. You all know I told you he was obsessed with the stock market. It seems he was over his daughters place and wanted to see the market results on TV. You know where the people on screen talk, and the ticker tape banner runs across the bottom of the screen. Well he wanted to change the station and couldn't find the remote.

However, his daughter's TV was one of those huge flat screens. It was permanently mounted on the wall. He had helped the husband mount it when it originally arrived. Well it seems Nicky was fiddling with the back of it to find where the manual controls were so he could change the stations without the remote. While he was fishing around the back of the set, he knocked it loose from the mounting. Unfortunately, it fell on him and landed on his chest knocking him down to the floor, crushing him to death. Remember, he only weighed about ninety pounds."

"Seems like you've been here way too long. You need to find another hobby. I think I'm going to stop carrying my gun around. It's not safe around my grand children, and besides I don't want you to be telling everyone that I died because the gun fell out of my pocket while I was reaching for change at the coffee shop, and it went off striking me in the head. You know too much about the people who come in here," said Smitty

"Isn't that the truth," added Cliff?

"I know, but when go home, and I get into to bed at night, my wife who loves me, calls me her baker man because I smell like fresh baked bread," said Rick

"So Rick, does that mean when YOU die you're not going to leave her any of your dough?" Robby laughs while all the men in the group roar with laughter, as Rick just smiles while stating. "Real funny. Real funny. You guys are a barrel of laughs!"

Cliff gets up from his seat and motions to Stan he wants to get going.

"Well I gotta go, it's getting late and I got a ton of tickets to write," Robby said.

"You guys all leaving me?" asks Rick.

"Well, come on Stan, I've got to go too," Cliff states.

"Yes, I know, it is getting late," replies Stan

Both Cliff and Stan get up and leave. Smitty starts to pack up his computer, and rises up from his seat. Rick looks up from his paper and watches as he unplugs the cord from the wall outlet and puts away his computer. He zips up the case and starts to rise, while grabbing his jacket.

"You going too?" asks Rick.

"Yes, I have to baby sit my grand children today."

"Well then I'll see you tomorrow?" states Rick.

"We'll see, not sure yet. See ya later."

The men all leave the shop, except for Rick, who is sitting there alone when a young woman enters the shop followed by a middle-aged man. Rick glances over at the woman and gives her the once over. She glances over at him and notices he is checking her out. She smiles.

"Hi! How ya doing, good to see ya," he says.

She nods and turns her attention back to the clerk behind the counter. Rick goes back to his paper. He picks it up and turns the page. He stretches it out in front of him, holding it up with both hands. "Whoa Boy!" he says as he looks out the front window of the shop, staring at nothing in particular, while waiting for the next person he knows to arrive. Then his gaze returns He looks around but no one has come in. He continues reading his paper, while saying "Whoa Boy!"

So here Rick sits. All alone except with the customers he does not know, and the shop personnel. He is enjoying life the way he wants to enjoy it. He's also making new friends as time goes by, but at the same time he is losing old ones too. They come into his life and they also leave. As he gets older year after year, he realizes that after he is gone there will be a new member to take his place, and they will tell stories about him, some serious, some humorous, but hopefully none tragic. So as he thinks these things through, with no one else there, he picks up his paper, and turns the page while stretching it out. He then utters his trademark saying with boredom and exasperation in his voice.........."Whoa Boy!"

The End

Disclaimer

All of the characters and occurrences contained herein are strictly the imagination of the author and are totally fictitious. Any similarities between characters and real persons either living or dead are mere coincidences'

Other Books by John Bourgeois

My Grandpa Fixes Stuff

Snow White and the Eighth Dwarf

Dungeon Rock, The Real Story

The Boys in the Window, the Play